SOUNDINGS IN THE THEOLOGY OF
OF
PSALMS

SOUNDINGS IN THE THEOLOGY OF

PSALMS

Perspectives and Methods in Contemporary Scholarship

Rolf A. Jacobson, editor

Fortress Press
Minneapolis

SOUNDINGS IN THE THEOLOGY OF PSALMS
Perspectives and Methods in Contemporary Scholarship

Cover image: *King David* by Anthony Armstrong
Cover design: Laurie Ingram
Book design: PerfecType, Nashville, TN

Library of Congress Cataloging-in-Publication Data

Soundings in the theology of Psalms : perspectives and methods in contemporary scholarship / Rolf A. Jacobson, editor.
    p. cm.
    Chiefly proceedings of the Book of Psalms Section of the Society of Biblical Literature at the society's 2008 annual meeting in Boston, Mass.
    Includes bibliographical references (p.   ) and indexes.
    ISBN 978-0-8006-9739-6 (alk. paper)
    1. Bible. O.T. Psalms—Criticism, interpretation, etc.—Congresses. I. Jacobson, Rolf A. II. Society of Biblical Literature. Book of Psalms Section. III. Society of Biblical Literature. Meeting (2008 : Boston, Mass.)
    BS1430.52.S63 2008
    223'.206—dc22

                                  2010018778

Manufactured in the U.S.A.

To Diane Jacobson and James Limburg

Contents

Preface

In the preface to his 1528 translation of the Psalter, Martin Luther wrote that the Psalter

> might well be called a little Bible. In it is comprehended most beautifully and briefly everything that is in the entire Bible. It is really a fine enchiridion or handbook. In fact, I have a notion that the Holy Spirit wanted to take the trouble himself to compile a short Bible and book of examples of all Christendom or all saints, so that anyone who could not read the whole Bible would have anyway almost an entire summary of it, comprised in one little book.[1]

Luther's oft-quoted description of the Psalter well illustrates both the ready accessibility of the book of Psalms as well as the deeply theological nature of its poems. The Psalms—filled with potent metaphors, raw cries of pain, clear confessions of faith, and joyous songs of praise—have been central to the life of faith because the people of God have had no trouble finding points of contact between these poems and their own lives. Moreover, God's people have not found those points of connection to be fleeting, shallow, or disappointing. Once tapped, the theological well of the Psalter does not go dry but rather becomes a flowing stream of living water to which believers long to return. The durability and accessibility of the Psalms has meant not only that believers have returned to them again and again as texts vital for the life of faith, but so too have theologians returned to the Psalms again and again as a source for reflection, wisdom, and revelation about the living God. In short, the psalms are both a source for faith and for theology—which is, after all, the systematic reflection on faith statements.

The present volume adds another chapter to the conversation about the theology of the book of Psalms. It does not seek to offer a definitive theology of the Psalms, but as indicated by the title of the series to which this volume belongs, it seeks various soundings regarding the theology of the Psalms. The essays by Jerome Creach, J. Clinton McCann, Beth Tanner, and myself first saw light as part of an invited session of the "Book of Psalms Section" of the Society of Biblical Literature at its 2008 annual meeting, in which participants were asked to address the question of the theology of the book of Psalms. Those essays were expanded and/or rewritten and now appear here in final form. Additional invitations were sent, and I was very pleased when Harry Nasuti, Nancy deClaissé-Walford, and Joel LeMon were also willing and able to contribute. Finally, Walter Brueggemann agreed to allow his seminal essay "The Psalms and the Life of Faith: A Suggested Typology of Function" to be reprinted, with the permission of Fortress Press, as part of the ongoing conversation.

In North America, the conversation surrounding the theology of the Psalms has largely been hosted by the Reformed tradition— one thinks of such luminaries as James Luther Mays, Bernhard Anderson, Patrick Miller, William Brown and, of course, Walter Brueggemann. The strong presence of Reformed voices in this volume (Brueggeman, Creach, McCann, and Tanner) bears further witness of how fruitful the conversation between Reformed theologians and the Psalms has been and continues to be. This volume also intentionally includes voices to represent other traditions. So added here are essays by a Wesleyan (Joel LeMon), a Roman

Catholic (Harry Nasuti), a Baptist (Nancy deClaissé-Walford), and a Lutheran (Rolf Jacobson). All of the scholars here write both as biblical theologians of the guild and as representatives of their own theological traditions. Invitations to scholars representing other traditions were also issued, but life circumstances did not permit them to participate in this round of the conversation.

I wish to express my gratitude to Victoria Smith, who helped with preparation of the manuscript, and to Neil Elliott at Fortress Press, without whose encouragement this volume would not have been finished. I also wish to thank the Society of Biblical Literature and especially the Book of Psalms Section for being the seedbed for scholarly research into the Psalms. I am also grateful for the colleagues whose essays appear here. Beth Tanner, Clint McCann, Harry Nasuti, Joel LeMon, Jerome Creach, Nancy deClaissé-Walford, and Walter Brueggemann are not only scholars and teachers for whom I have great respect, they are friends whom I love. Working with them on these essays has been for me an experience of divine grace—an instance, to borrow again from Luther, of the "mutual conversation of brothers and sisters" as a means of God's grace (*Smalcald Articles* 3.4). This volume is dedicated to my first two teachers in the Psalms—Diane Jacobson and James Limburg. Both are prime examples that the promise of Psalm 1 is trustworthy. They have spent their lives sinking their roots deep into the life-giving water of the Word of the Lord. In all they have done, they have prospered.

Contributors

Walter Brueggemann
Columbia Seminary

Jerome F. D. Creach
Pittsburgh Theological Seminary

Nancy L. deClaissé-Walford
McAfee School of Theology, Mercer University

Rolf A. Jacobson
Luther Seminary

Joel M. LeMon
Candler School of Theology, Emory University

J. Clinton McCann Jr.
Eden Theological Seminary

Harry P. Nasuti
Fordham University

Beth Tanner
New Brunswick Theological Seminary

CHAPTER 1

The Psalms and the Life of Faith: A Suggested Typology of Function

Walter Brueggemann

W hat has been the function and intention of the Psalms as they were shaped, transmitted, and repeatedly used?[1] That is, what was the purpose of "doing them," albeit in highly stylized fashion?

What was being done when the Psalms were "done"? Such questions move in a constructive direction, in contrast to the more analytic questions of form and setting. To ask about the function of the Psalms means to move away from direct textual evidence and to engage in some tentative reconstructions. Our consideration of function must of course be based on the best judgments we have about form and setting in life.[2] The present discussion assumes and fully values both the methods and the gains of form-critical study. I am proposing neither a criticism nor a displacement of form-critical work. Rather, I explore the possibility of a move beyond form criticism that necessarily is concerned with hermeneutical issues.

The main questions and conclusions about form in the Psalms have largely been laid down by Hermann Gunkel. As the reviews of Ronald Clements and Erhard Gerstenberger make clear, we have not moved very far from Gunkel's fivefold classification, even though there is still room for refinement regarding those psalms

that do not fall into Gunkel's major categories.[3] Claus Westermann has attempted some consolidation of Gunkel's classification, and we will have more to say about his way of putting the
matter.[4]

Questions of setting in life for the Psalms are much more
unsettled.[5] Concerning the hymns, there has been some uneasi-
ness with the festival hypothesis of Sigmund Mowinckel, perhaps
because it has been judged too comprehensive, explaining too
much in too singular a way.[6] On the other hand, Westermann has
largely dissolved the question of setting in life, so that it is mean-
ingless. Thus he says of the hymn, "The life setting is the experience
of God's intervention in history,"[7] a judgment that has no interest
in the sociology or social function of the hymn. So, concerning
the hymn, we are still left mainly with some form of the festival hypothesis.[8] Concerning the setting in life of the lament, and
especially the individual lament, the judgment of Hans Schmidt
(made already in 1928) has led to a major strand of interpretation that sets the lament in the temple, in a juridical context of
the innocently accused who seek vindication and plead for acquit-
tal.[9] Schmidt's general understanding has been refined by Walter
Beyerlin and Lienhard Delekat, but not greatly advanced.[10] An
alternative hypothesis by Gerstenberger breaks the linkage with
the temple and with the juridical frame.[11] He proposes that we
have in the individual lament reflections of a domestic ritual of
rehabilitation conducted by the legitimate and recognized, though
lay, leaders in the community. They deal with those whose lives, for
whatever reason, have disintegrated.

Gerstenberger removes the ritual and the Psalms from the temple
and thinks they may have been used in the home. On the question
of setting in life (and derivatively of function), Gerstenberger is
more helpful than Westermann, for even with his acute analysis
of form and structure, Westermann is not in fact interested in the
institutional setting. By contrast, Gerstenberger suggests a cogent
sociological situation.[12]

I

While form-critical work, especially with reference to setting, is not dormant, we may regard the present consensus as fairly stable. It is in any case firm enough to provide a basis from which to consider the question of *function*. One can of course answer the question of function by saying that the function was to lament and to praise. But in addition to being simply a tautology, such an answer stays in the realm of religion, where interpretation has stayed too long. However, to ask about function permits us to approach the matter from other, more pragmatic perspectives. We may consider the issue of the social usefulness of the Psalms that influence the character and quality of social existence. Two purposes may be served by asking the question this way. First, it may advance our understanding of Israel's intention in transmitting the Psalms. Second, it may help contemporary users to identify more clearly what resources are available in the use of the Psalms and what may be "done" in this "doing" of them. I suggest a convergence of a *contemporary pastoral agenda* with a more *historical exegetical interest*. Thus the question of function is put as a hermeneutical issue.

The question concerns both the use in ancient Israel, which admits of some scholarly analysis of the Psalms, and the contemporary religious use of the Psalms by practitioners of faith.[13] The hold that the Psalms have on the contemporary practice of faith and piety is a legitimate part of our concern. That hold is evident liturgically, with regular and sustained use of the Psalms in the daily office generation after generation. It is also evident devotionally, in those free church traditions that are not so keen on liturgic use but nurture persons in their own prayer life to draw guidance and strength from the Psalms.

And finally, contemporary use is evident pastorally, for many pastors find in the Psalms remarkable and reliable resources for many situations, the hospital call being paradigmatic. Thus, liturgical, devotional, and pastoral uses are dimensions of the contemporary function of the Psalms.

In this discussion, we hazard the provisional presupposition that modern and ancient uses of the Psalms share a common intent and function, even though other matters such as setting and institution may be different.[14] We may anticipate a *commonality of function* even when other matters diverge. That commonality, I suggest, is probable because the psalms (and especially the most poignant of them) present human persons in situations of regression: when they are most vulnerable in hurt, most ecstatic in naive joy, most sensitized to life, driven to the extremities of life and faith, when all the "covers" of modern rationality or ancient convention have disappeared or become dysfunctional. The hermeneutical possibility of moving back and forth between ancient function and contemporary intentionality exists because the use of the Psalms in every age is for times when the most elemental and raw human issues are in play.[15] The intended function and resilient practice of the Psalms reflect their peculiar capacity to be present to those elemental and raw human issues.

In what follows, I make special appeal to the work of Paul Ricoeur.[16] He has for some time studied the role of language in the life of faith. Out of the juxtaposition of the Psalms and the work of Ricoeur come fresh suggestions concerning the function of the Psalms.

II

Ricoeur understands the dynamic of life as a movement, dialectic but not regular or patterned, of disorientation and reorientation.[17] The human organism struggles to maintain some kind of equilibrium in his or her life. That sense of holistic orientation, of being "at home," is a gift that is given and not forced, yet we struggle to it, fight for it, resist losing it, and regularly deny its loss when it is gone. Two movements in human life are important: (1) deep reluctance to let loose of a world that has passed away, and (2) capacity to embrace a new world being given. These themes in Ricoeur's study will be important to interpretation of the Psalms suggested here.

Human experience includes those dangerous and difficult times of dislocation and disorientation when the sky does fall and the world does indeed come to an end. The figure of disorientation may be taken psychologically and sociologically. It includes all facets of our common life and experience. The times of disorientation are those when persons are driven to the *extremities* of emotion, of integrating capacity, and of language. In the company of Isaiah, we are "undone" (Isa 6:5). There is no speech, and there is no safe reality about which to speak. The loss of an orderly life is linked to a loss of language, or at least to a discovery of the inadequacy of conventional language.[18]

Human persons are not meant for situations of disorientation. They will struggle against such situations with all their energies. Insofar as persons are hopeful and healthy, they may grow and work through to a new orientation. But as Freud has seen, human persons are mostly inclined to look back, to grasp for old equilibria, to wish for them, and to deny that they are gone. Ricoeur, in his study of Freud, is clear that it is *situations of dislocation* that evoke the dangerous language of extremity, which may express *hope* but more likely resistance.

The countermovement of reorientation comes, says Ricoeur, through a representation of reality that is genuinely new and has the mark of gift.[19] The reorientation has both continuities with and discontinuities from what has been. But the accent is on the new. It is a surprise. In our resistance, we do not expect to be surprised. The new situation is not an achievement or a working out of the dislocation but a newness that comes to us. Equally, it is not a "passage," as though it were automatic or inevitable.[20] It comes as miracle wrought from outside the situation. And it is only when that newness meets the human person or community convincingly that an abandonment of old orientation may be fully affirmed.

I propose that the sequence of *orientation-disorientation-reorientation* is a helpful way to understand the use and function of the Psalms. Very likely, the overview suggested here has been intentional in the practice of many believing people, even though they have not recognized or articulated it in this way.

1. *The Psalms of Orientation.* The psalms we include here are not the most interesting, for there is in them no great movement, no tension to resolve. Indeed, what mainly characterizes them is the absence of tension. The mindset and worldview of those who enjoy a serene location of their lives are characterized by a sense of the orderliness, goodness, and reliability of life. Thus, they might be especially represented in *creation psalms* that reflect the coherence of life:

> These all look to you,
> to give them their food in due season.
> When you give to them, they gather it up;
>   when you open your hand,
> they are filled with good things. (Ps 104:27-28)

Or reference may be made to the psalms that teach clear, reliable retribution, in which evil is punished and good is rewarded (e.g., Psalms 1 and 119). Reference to creation and retribution suggests that psalms of orientation especially relate to sapiential tradition, which, as Robert Gordis and Brian Kovacs have suggested, reflects a class orientation of those who enjoy and appreciate much of life's material goodness.[21]

We might better seek examples in the book of Proverbs, which largely reflects life in its coherence and reliability. Apparently, Psalm 37 is a sapiential statement in the book of Psalms that reflects undisturbed, uncritical equilibrium. It offers imperatives and prohibitions about how to maintain and enhance this order. It asserts Yahweh's reliability and makes a didactic contrast with the wicked.

Psalm 145 might be located in this grouping. It may be regarded as a not very interesting collection of clichés. But in fact, it affirms God's providential care. The unimaginative style makes the confident claim. Such a psalm comes very close to civil religion, for it sounds like a celebration of the status quo. The other element that could easily be placed here are some of the psalms of ascent (e.g., 127; 128; 131; 133) reflecting domestic life that is in good order. They are the voice of genuine gratitude and piety for such rich blessings.[22]

It may be legitimate to place here what Westermann calls descriptive hymns,[23] for they anticipate or remember no change. They describe how things are, with the assurance that they are well grounded and with the anticipation that they will continue.[24] The function of such description is the continued reaffirmation and reconstruction of this good world. Thus songs of creation, wisdom, retribution, and blessing all function in this same context of good order and well-being.

2. *The Psalms of Disorientation.* The psalms of lament, both individual and corporate, are ways of entering linguistically into a new distressful situation in which the old orientation has collapsed. There are various shapes and nuances of distress in different psalms, suggesting that different ones are appropriate for use depending on how fully the subject has *accepted and embraced* the dislocation and how much *resistance or denial* remains.

Thus, some of the psalms remember better times (Ps 42:4) back in the old period of orientation. There is a wish to return to that situation. Others are heavy in anger and resentment against the one who has caused disorientation. (It does not greatly matter if that one is thought to be God or enemies.) This mood leaves the impression that the speaker believes that the loss of orientation is reversible and the old orientation is retrievable.

Westermann has most helpfully shown that the Psalms move from petition and plea to praise.[25] And Gerstenberger has argued that the form of Israel's speech is complaint and not lament; that is, protest and not resignation. There is expectation and even insistence that Yahweh can be moved to act and that Yahweh will act.[26] And when Yahweh acts, Yahweh will bring things to a new life-order. The break between plea and praise in the Psalms reflects an important moment of realism.[27] There is a turn from yearning for the old orientation, a recognition that it is gone and not retrievable, and a readiness for a new orientation. The conclusion of vow, praise, and "assurance of being heard" faces forward. They have put the old lost world behind. Thus, whatever the spoken or acted device of the "turn," the movement reflects a firm resolve to look in a new direction. There is a turn from resentful remembering to a fresh anticipation of an equilibrium that is a gift from God, genuinely new and not a restatement of the old.[28] In speaking of that remarkable turn, Ricoeur writes, "Remembrance gives rise to anticipation; archaism gives rise to prophecy."[29] The turn is a move beyond remembering. But it could not be done without the painful part of remembering. In the various psalms of lament and in the various parts of these psalms, the speaker is located at various places in the movement of living into and emerging out of disorientation.

Two specific comments are in order. First, if the psalms of *lament* correlate with the situation of *displacement*, we may have a fresh appreciation for some metaphors often used—for example, "pit," and the various references to "enemy." This rich array of language in which the words tumble out becomes, then, not an exegetical problem to be solved but a pastoral opportunity to let the impressionistic speech touch the particular circumstance of dislocation. For the truth of the matter is that the listener to such a psalm in a time of actual dislocation will have no doubt as to the meaning of the references and will find such exegetical speculation both unnecessary and distracting. To fall into "the pit" is indeed to lose one's old equilibrium. The "enemy" is quite obviously the one who has caused the loss. David Clines has seen that the identity of the Suffering Servant of Second Isaiah is not a code to be cracked but an open-ended statement that allows for and encourages multiple interpretations.[30]

Using Clines's insight, I suggest that a person in disorientation is precisely the one who has the freedom and vitality to face the openness of lament language. Those who are safe and settled in an old equilibrium are the ones who want to identify the enemy and all the other figures in this poetry. Interpreters must be freed of our closely oriented habits of exegesis if the psalm is to have the freedom to fully articulate the experience of disorientation. That is, the function of the psalm requires of us a certain imaginative freedom of interpretation.

Second, special reference may be made to Psalm 88. So far as I know, Westermann nowhere deals with this psalm as an important exception to the "plea/praise" pattern. Nor does Gerstenberger, to my knowledge, deal with this as a lament rather than as a complaint.[31] Perhaps it is the exception that proves the rule. But it is in fact the case that Psalm 88 is unrelieved in its embrace of disorientation: there is no movement away from displacement. It includes "I" statements of trouble (vv. 3-5), three "Thou" statements of accusation, and a middle section of rhetorical questions (vv. 10-14). But the questions do not linger for an answer. The psalm concludes in verses 15-18 in utter hopelessness. I submit that this psalm has a peculiar and distinctive function and is a resource as precious as it is peculiar.

3. *The Psalms of Reorientation.* Concerning these, we may provisionally follow Westermann's consolidation of hymns and songs of thanksgiving, to group them together as songs of celebration concerning reorientation. I am aware that Westermann has not been widely followed. And it may be that in terms of form, the two different types cannot be coupled. But in terms of function, declarative hymns and thanksgiving songs do agree in the welcome and amazed recognition that a newness has been given that is not achieved, not automatic, and not derived from the old, but is rather a genuine newness wrought by gift. Thus, Westermann's proposal may be open to question in terms of form but is functionally on target.

We may group hymns and songs of thanksgiving together. However, as indicated, we need to distinguish between declarative and descriptive hymns in terms of function. Thus, we may be left with two functions as well as two forms, but they must be grouped differently with reference to form and function:

    a. The two clusters of *form* may be:
        1. hymns, both descriptive and declarative, and
        2. songs of thanksgiving.
    b. The two clusters of *function* may be:

1. songs of orientation, including descriptive hymns, and
2. songs of reorientation, including declarative hymns and songs of thanksgiving.

There is no need to force the issue from function to form. It is sufficient to acknowledge that groupings will be different for function and for form. Thus, descriptive hymns, as Westermann has seen, describe an enduring state of things and therefore reflect a continuing secure orientation. By contrast, the declarative hymns and songs of thanksgiving do not *describe* what has been but assert what has just now been wrought. This function speaks of surprise and wonder, miracle and amazement, when a new orientation has been granted to the disoriented for which there was no ground for expectation.

These psalms reflect a quite new circumstance that speaks of newness (it is not the old revived); surprise (there was no ground in the disorientation to anticipate it); and gift (it is not given by the lamenter). For these reasons, this new circumstance evokes and requires a celebration, for reversals must be celebrated (see Luke 15:6-7, 9-10, 22-24, 32).[32] Psalms scholarship has worked hard at characterizing what this celebration is. The three dominant hypotheses are those of Sigmund Mowinckel, Artur Weiser, and Hans-Joachim Kraus; respectively, enthronement festival, covenant renewal, and royal Zion festival.[33] Each of these suggestions obviously has some warrant. But perhaps the vitality of this celebration is not to be understood in terms of Babylonian parallels (so Mowinckel), in terms of Israel's traditions (so Weiser), or with reference to Jerusalem's institution (so Kraus). Perhaps we may stay with the rich and diverse human experience of reorientation, of which more than one language can speak. And while the form or legitimacy of the festival may come from a borrowed phrase such as "Yahweh is king," the power, vitality, and authority for celebration come from the unarguable experience of those persons who have discovered that the world has come to an end but a new creation is given. Life has disintegrated but has been formed miraculously again.[34]

The enduring authority of these psalms must surely be found in their ability to touch the *extremities* of human life, extremities we have characterized in terms of disorientation and reorientation. The extremity of reorientation is as shattering as that of disorientation.

Thus, Westermann, in defending his two-type hypothesis, can quote Gunkel: "In the alternation between lament and song of thanks there unrolls the whole life of the pious."[35] It may be added that songs of orientation present a dimension of life not characterized by extremity. Thus, the psalms Westermann labels as descriptive and declarative stand at the far moments of orientation and reorientation and should not be grouped together in terms of function.

III

Ricoeur has for some time been in dialogue with Sigmund Freud. Behind that has been his attempt to understand the conflict between two hermeneutical perspectives and his attempt to find a way to face them both.[36] On the one hand, Ricoeur has tried to take seriously what he calls the "hermeneutic of suspicion," represented by Karl Marx, Freud, and Friedrich Nietzsche.[37] It is the purpose of this approach to expose the dishonesty of interested speech that protests, conceals, and controls and to be attentive to the deceptions (especially self-deceptions) that are practiced in the name of truth. In Marxist terms, it means discerning the distance between appearance and reality. In Freudian terms, it means paying attention to the ways in which reality is suppressed and driven into the unconscious. In a word, this is an unmasking that is aware that every statement is an attempt to mislead and misrepresent.[38]

The other hermeneutical tradition (to which Ricoeur is more drawn by his interest in language) is that of full symbolization. This tradition holds that the oversurplus of language permits more to be said than the original articulation intended, and it assumes that attentive listening can always hear more in freighted texts. Ricoeur refers to this as "iconic augmentation."[39] This tradition of interpretation is represented by the *sensus plenior* of the Roman Catholic tradition, the New Hermeneutic, and the obscure possibilities of structuralism.[40] Ricoeur understands the work of this hermeneutic to be re-presentation, to state with fullness the old realities of sacred coherence in ways that are especially appropriate to, and run beyond, the sober meaning of words.[41]

Now it is clear that these two approaches are in some tension. I cite two specific examples. First, Loretta Dornisch observes that in Scripture study, traditional biblical hermeneutics is concerned with representation—that is, restatement of the claim of the text in its full kerygmatic power—whereas historical criticism is a practice of the hermeneutic of suspicion, which wants to penetrate back to what was "really there originally."[42] Presently, it is recognized that this posture of critical, historical study creates new and different issues for those engaged in Scripture study in the environs of a believing community.[43] And, therefore, Brevard Childs's title is important, ". . . Old Testament as *Scripture*."

Second, and more personally, I have had conversation with a pastor whom I most respect who is an accomplished Freudian therapist. He is aware, on the one hand, of the very difficult task of being a therapist of the critical, suspicionist tradition; that is, to practice consistently that no words really say what they mean and must be exposed as deceptive. On the other hand, he is at the same time a faithful Christian preacher who regularly must speak these large words about the truth of the gospel without turning the same suspicionist eye on those words until there are no words left to speak. The struggle to hold these together is difficult for any who would believe honestly.

Ricoeur argues that these two hermeneutics are both essential and must be seen in a dialectic of *displacement* and *recapture*:

> Consequently, the first task—the displacement—cannot be separated from the second task—the recapture of meaning in interpretation. This alternation of relinquishing (*déprise*) and recapture (*reprise*) is the philosophical basis of the entire metapsychology.[44]

It is precisely the *dispossession* of false and deceptive positions that can lead to the *recovery* of powerful symbols. Thus, the two works that must both be carried on are (1) the criticism of idols, and (2) heeding the true God who will make all things new.[45] Ricoeur's discernment of these two hermeneutical positions can be correlated with the paradigm of psalmic function I have proposed above. Thus, the hermeneutic of suspicion is practiced in the lament songs of dislocation, and the hermeneutic of representation is practiced in the celebrative songs of relocation. (I leave to one side the settled songs of orientation, but I believe that at times they may assert the new and at other times stand in need of the radical criticism of suspicion.) Ricoeur's model can help in understanding both what is going on in the text of the Psalms and what is going on in the life of the user(s) of the psalms, for as Ricoeur argues, it is the experience of limit that is important to the expression of limit.[46] The psalms of disorientation and reorientation may be regarded as expressions of limit. That is, they speak about times when normalcy is sharply in question. The user(s) brings to the psalms experiences of limit. Thus, the use and intention of a psalm depend on this hermeneutic coincidence between what is at issue in the text of the psalm and what is at issue in the life of the user(s).

The lament *psalms of dislocation* may be understood as an instance of the *hermeneutic of suspicion.*[47] The lament psalm of dislocation becomes necessary usually quite unexpectedly. It is necessary in a situation in which the old worldview, old faith presuppositions, and old language are no longer adequate. Obviously, if one has (in practice or even implicitly) been living out of creation songs about stability and harmony in life, or songs of morality about the equity of life, then one cannot readily receive abrasions and incongruities that provide the kind of data such songs cannot contain and comprehend. That experience of radical dissonance is what is presented to us in the laments. They are speeches of surprised dismay and disappointment, for the speaker never expected this to happen to him or her. They are fresh utterances, sharp ejaculations by people accustomed either to the smooth songs of equilibrium or to not saying anything at all because things are "all right." They are the shrill speeches of those who suddenly discover that they are trapped and the water is rising and the sun may not come up tomorrow in all its benevolence. And we are betrayed!

These psalms are the voices of those who find their circumstance dangerously, and not just inconveniently, changed. And they do not like it. These are the speeches of caged men and women getting familiar with their new place, feeling the wall for a break, hunting in the dark for hidden weapons, testing the nerve and patience of those who have perpetrated the wrong. We may observe two features of this poetry in particular.

First, we should not expect the speaker of Psalm 37 or Psalm 145 ever to speak a cross word. However, it is likely that the speakers of harsh laments are the same voices as the singers of hymns, but in radically new circumstances. Now the same voices speak venom against God, enemies, parents, and everyone else, venom they did not know they had in their bodies. But consistent with the hermeneutic of suspicion, this is because the facade of convention and well-being has at last been penetrated. The beast is permitted an appearance.

The speakers of these psalms are in a vulnerable, regressed situation in which the voice of desperate, fear-filled, hate-filled reality is unleashed and no longer covered by the niceties of conventional sapiential teaching. As in the freedom of speech in therapy of regression, any language and any speech are appropriate. So also in lament psalms, and most unmistakably in the laments of Job,[48] anything may and will be said. The juices flow, and the animal is loose.

Perhaps the acceptance of the animal role illuminates why the speaker is presented as surrounded by other animals who will devour, for the speaker is now able to face the censured imagery of beastliness in his or her own person (Pss 7:2; 22:13-14, 16; 57:4; 58:6; 59:6; 74:19). The speaker discovers that she or he is also a beast once the conventions have been penetrated. So in Psalm 73, when life is inequitable, the speaker is aware of a skewed relationship in which one is less than human:

When my soul was embittered,
    when I was pricked in heart,
I was stupid and ignorant;
I was like a brute beast toward you. (Ps 73:21-22; cf. 102:7-8)[49]

The speaker discovers animal dimensions in life. Only now he or she is not king of the jungle, as in Psalm 37.

Second, these complaints are filled with questions:

You have kept count of my tossings;
    put my tears in your bottle.
    Are they not in your record? (Ps 56:8)

In God I trust; I am not afraid.
    What can a mere mortal do to me? (Ps 56:11)

Have you not rejected us, O God? (Ps 60:10)

Will you hide yourself forever? (Ps 89:46)

Why have you forsaken us these many days . . . ,
    unless you have utterly rejected us,
    and are angry with us beyond measure[?] (Lam 5:20, 22)

These questions are usually understood as motivations to get Yahweh to do something. They are clearly rhetorical questions that do not seem to expect an answer. Or perhaps the answer is thought to be so obvious that it needs no expression. They may be only raw expressions of emotion. But they may also be understood as questions now occurring to the speaker for the first time: bold new thoughts, the answers to which are as yet unknown, for the question is now first posed in the mouth of the disoriented.[50] The poet, in the collapse of convention, permits regression to deep questions never before permitted and until now censured by the community and by self. They are the "ah-ha's" of a dangerous kind; they go to the brink for the first time to ask, "What if . . . ?" What if the whole orientation is a fraud that can no longer be relied on? And once asked, such a probing can never be unasked. The disorientation, once brought to full speech, is irreversible.

It is the function of these songs, if seen this way, to enable, require, and legitimate the complete rejection of the old orientation. That old arrangement is seen, if not as fraud, at least as inadequate to the new circumstance. The Psalms have the abrasive effect of dismantling the old systems that hide the well-off from the dangerous theological realities of life. It is a key insight of Freud that until there is an embrace of honest helplessness, there is no true gospel that can be heard. Until the idols have been exposed, there is no chance of the truth of the true God. It is telling that these psalms use the words "pit/Sheol/waters/depths," for in therapy, one must be "in the depths" if there is to be new life.[51] Freud has seen that the utter abandonment of pretense is a prerequisite to new joy. (The loss/finding, death/life dynamic is evident also in the three celebrations of Luke 15.)

These psalms, correlated with a hermeneutic of suspicion, warn against an easy hermeneutic of symbols and myths or an easy psychology of growth through symbolization. These psalms mean to empty out the old symbols that have failed.[52] They apparently know that the dismantling must be complete and without reserve. And if the dismantling is not total, the religious building of life likely will be a construction of idols. Thus, Psalm 88 stands as singularly important, for it is a word precisely at the bottom of the pit when every hope is abandoned. The speaker is alone, and there is as yet no hint of dawn. Psalm 88 is the full recognition of collapse.[53]

Conversely, a similar correlation may be suggested between the *psalms of celebration* (declarative hymns and songs of thanksgiving) and the *hermeneutic of recollection and representation*. The song celebrative of reorientation is a movement out of the disorientation marked by lament. In a parallel way, the critical hermeneutic of suspicion is superseded (in a dialectical fashion, to be sure) by the restorative hermeneutic of representation. The song of celebration is a new song sung at the appearance of a new reality, new creation, new harmony, new reliability (Pss 33:3; 40:3; 96:1; 98:1; 144:9; 149:1; Isa 42:10; Rev 14:3). Its style and rhetoric must speak of the quality of surprise and newness that are appropriate to such new reality, which may be variously symbolized. It may, indeed, with Mowinckel, be enthronement of a new king, fresh confidence that there is a life-giving order operative among us. It may be articulated, with Weiser, as new covenant, as belonging to a community bound to and cared for by God. It may be, with Kraus, affirmation of the primal, sacral institutions, dynasty, and temple. But the reality of the new experience is something other than, and more than, what can be caught in and confined by any one of these referents. It is the experience that the world has new coherence, that the devastating hopelessness of the lament is not finally appropriate for the way life is. Thus it is telling that the "new song" occurs not only in the great hymns of enthronement (96:1; 98:1) or even concerning the king (144:9), but also in the thanksgiving of 33:3 and 40:3, which may refer to any personal crisis.

As the hermeneutic reflected in the lament is, following Ricoeur's words, "reductive and demystifying," so this hermeneutic is "restorative, recollective of the sacred," daring to represent in fresh form the elemental well-being first articulated by the primal myths.[54]

Thus, the declarative hymns and songs of thanksgiving speak of a newness not unlike the old assurances expressed in the descriptive psalms "before the flood." It may be for that reason that the mythic dimension is more explicit, daring, and comprehensive in the hymns than in the laments. The songs of celebration wish to take the worshiper not back into the old primal ordering of goodness (as in Gen 1:31) but into a newness now being given. The hymns thus look back in mythic categories and out of them assert a promissory conviction.[55] As the laments want to show life—in its shattered leanness—as regression to primal chaos, so the celebrative songs tend to be effusive with a surplus of meaning in every metaphor and symbol.

It is likely that the hymns can scarcely be overinterpreted. The new song asserts that the waters will not drown and the pit did not hold, that the captor was unnerved and the enemy is shattered. The sky has fallen but is now secured again. The world has ended but begun again. And there is no word for that beyond doxology.[56]

Just as the lament warned against celebration too quickly, and just as the hermeneutic of suspicion warns us against positive symbolization too easily and early, so now our discernment leads us in the opposite direction. Israel has the capacity to exploit the fullness of language in the service of reorientation and new creation. Such a practice affirms that we do not need to be forever reductive, demystifying, critical, and exposing. There is a time when this work is done.

Unmasking has run its course when life is shaken from its phoniness and scattered in its deception. Then it is appropriate to turn to the gathering work of symbols.[57] Or to move from hermeneutic to the Psalms, Israel must not forever lament, complain, protest, and question. There is a time for affirmation and rejoicing, a time to end the criticism, to receive the gift, and to sing a doxology (see Eccl 3:2-10).[58]

Thus, our appeal to Ricoeur suggests correlations between functions of the Psalms and two alternative hermeneutics, which correspond to two extremities of life.

1. The movement of our life, if we are attentive, is the movement of *orientation*, *disorientation*, and *reorientation*. And in our daily pilgrimage, we use much of our energy for this work.

2. This experience is correlated with songs of orientation (descriptive hymns), *songs of disorientation* (laments), and *songs of reorientation* (declarative hymns). While declarative and descriptive hymns may be grouped together form-critically, they stand at the opposite extremes of Israel's experience of life and of God.

3. The descriptive and declarative hymns—as opposites—form an envelope for the closer movement in the individual lament itself. Following Westermann's analysis, the two parts of the lament, plea and praise, express in microcosm the movement we have been discussing. The plea still looks back to the old orientation, still yearning for it and grudging its loss, while the praise element begins to look forward and to anticipate. Thus, the two parts of the lament—one of which looks back in anger and chagrin and the other forward in hope—correlate with our two hermeneutical postures. The lament as plea and petition regresses to the oldest

fears, the censured questions, the deepest hates, the unknown and unadmitted venom, and a yearning; whereas the lament as praise anticipates and is open to gift. It looks ahead, consents to receive, and intends to respond in gratitude.[59] The two functions, as the two hermeneutics, belong together. So Ricoeur can speak of the two together as regressive-progressive in a way whereby the remembrance gives rise to anticipation.[60] He sees the two as linked and the process as "inherently dialectical."[61]

4. In one other articulation of the same, Ricoeur suggests a difference between the second naïveté and the first.[62] The first naïveté is the precritical. It believes everything, indeed too much. It is an enjoyment of well-being but unaware of oppression and incongruity. It is a glad reception of community, but unaware of hurt. It can afford to be uncritical because everything makes sense. But growth—and indeed life—means moving to criticism: a new awareness of self in conflict, of others in dishonest interestedness, of God in enmity. The critical dimension of our pilgrimage discovers, with Marx, the slippage between appearance and reality in our social arrangements, slippage poorly covered by ideology. And it discovers, with Freud, the censorship that we exercise and that is exercised on us.

But the second naïveté is postcritical, not precritical. The second naïveté has been through the pit and is now prepared to "hope all things" (1 Cor 13:7). But now, hope is after the pit. It now knows that finally things have been reduced and need be reduced no more. It knows that our experience is demystified, as it must be. But it knows that even in a world demystified and reduced, grace intrudes and God makes all things new. The ones who give thanks and sing genuinely new songs must be naive or they would not bother to sing songs and to give thanks. But it is a praise in which the anguish of disorientation is not forgotten, removed, or absent.

IV

Through all of this, I have been appealing to Ricoeur's theory of language.[63] Clearly, of all the points I have attempted to utilize, it is language that interests Ricoeur the most. In general, his work is related to the New Hermeneutic and its discernment of language. For this, we may refer to the enigmatic statements of Ernst Fuchs and Gerhard Ebeling[64] and to the extended discussion of Hans-Georg Gadamer.[65] More directly, we may refer to the studies of Robert Funk and John Dominic Crossan on New Testament parables.[66] And closest to our concern are the shrewd conclusions drawn by David Clines concerning Isaiah 53. This general movement sees that alongside language that describes what is, there is a language that evokes what is not. Thus, this language has a creative function. It does not simply follow reality and reflect it, but it leads reality to become what it is not. So we may appeal to Martin Heidegger's well-known aphorism, "The poet is the shepherd of being."[67] But we should insist that for Israel, the matter is much more characterized in promissory ways than Heidegger seems to suggest.[68] The relation of language and reality is dialectical. New reality permits new language; language spoken by Israel's Authoritative Speaker calls forth new reality. In his own study, Ricoeur has illustrated this with particular reference (1) to the *proverb*, which has been a description of conventional reality (i.e., before the disorientation, but which is now turned to surprise); (2) to the *eschatological saying*, which is no longer interpreted literally but now used to rediscern present reality; and (3) to the *parable*, which is not a teaching of general ethical truth but a surprise that causes a new awareness of reality. Each of these, he has shown, is presented to evoke a scandalous perception of reality that breaks our conventions.[69]

This creative, evocative function of language is precisely what is at work in the Psalms.[70] The Psalms transmit to us ways of speaking that are appropriate to the extremities of human experience as known concretely in Israel. Or, to use Ricoeur's language, we have "limit-expressions" (laments, songs of celebration) that match "limit-experiences" (disorientation, reorientation). The use of the Psalms in one's own life and in ministry depends on making a genuine and sensitive match between expression and experience. The enduring authority of this language stems from the fact that it bears witness to common human experience but is at the same time practiced in this concrete community with specific memories and hopes. Thus the openness to the universal and the passion for the concrete come together in these poems.

Without such a view of language, the psalms of extremity are reduced to clichés, at best a ready standing supply of words that can be conventionally drawn on to stylize things. To view the Psalms that way is to trivialize them, as I believe has widely happened and is perhaps even encouraged by our inability to get beyond rather academic categories of presentation.

We have asked about the function of the Psalms. I should argue (in Ricoeur's terms of *demystifying* and *representing*) that the function of the Psalms is twofold. First, the Psalms bring human experience to sufficiently vivid expression so that it may be embraced as the real situation in which persons must live. This applies equally to the movement in the life of an individual person and to the public discernment of new reality. Persons and communities are not fully present in a situation of disorientation until it has been brought to speech. One may in fact be there but absent to the situation by denial and self-deception. Specifically, until the reality of "the pit" is spoken about, with all its hatred of enemies, its mistrust of God, its fear of "beasts," its painful yearning for old, better times, its daring questions of dangerous edges—until all that is brought to speech— it is likely that one will continue to assume the old, now-discredited, dysfunctional equilibrium that, in fact, is powerless. Living in the "old equilibrium" that is powerless makes one numb, mute, liable to oppression, and easily used by others.[71] But to speak first the words to the disoriented, and then to have the disoriented actually speak the words, can be a new recognition and embrace of the actual situation. The censorship of the old orientation is so strong that the actual situation may be denied and precluded. The "language event" of the lament thus permits movement beyond *naïveté* and acceptance of one's actual situation *critically*.

The songs of new orientation perform a parallel work. Those who have entered deeply into "the pit" may presume that is the

permanent situation, when, in fact, life has moved on and their circumstances have been transformed toward newness. In such times,
the songs of celebration may lead the person or community to
embrace the context of newness in which they live.

Second, the language of these poems does more than just help
persons to embrace and recognize their real situation. In dramatic
and dynamic ways, the songs can also function to evoke and form
new realities that did not exist until, or apart from, the actual singing of the song. Thus, the speech of the new song does not just
recognize what is given but evokes it, calls it into being, forms it.
Israel's hymnic assertion, "Yahweh is king," is not just a description
of Yahweh the king, but evokes Yahweh to kingship. It calls Yahweh
to the throne. Thus, understood in a quite different way, the old
claims of Mowinckel concerning the creative, evocative function of
hymns to bring forth a new reality are reaffirmed.

Ricoeur is repetitious and clear on this point. The redescription
of human reality in terms of positive celebration is not regressive,
not a return to an old, safe, religious world where God was on the
throne. A return to the primal symbols must therefore be treated
"suspiciously." The redescription of reality in terms of positive celebration has a lament behind it that decisively cuts it off from the
primal. There is no return.[72] The second creation is a new one and
not a return to the first one. Thus, the hymn of celebration is not
regressive but anticipatory.[73] So we may say of the doxologies, as
Ricoeur says of good art sketches, that they are

> not simply projections of the artist's conflicts, but the sketches
> of the solution. Dreams look backward to infancy, the past. The
> work of art goes ahead of the artist; it is a prospective symbol of
> his personal synthesis and of man's future, rather than a regressive
> symbol of his unresolved conflicts.[74]

Ricoeur follows Ernest Jones in observing that symbols have
two vectors. They "repeat our childhood in all the senses, chronolog-
ical and non-chronological, of that childhood. On the other hand,
they explore our adult life."[75] So it is with the songs of celebration.

The hymn (even more than the song of thanksgiving) goes ahead. It goes ahead of the poet, of the worshiper, of the pastor. It calls into being the new creation, and there are glimpses—only glimpses—of life in the new kingdom in which all other gods have been destroyed and we have only to do with the lover of justice (Ps 99:4). The new song is sung (Rev 14:3). It is a song about the new king (Rev 14:7), but it is also about the death of Babylon (Rev 14:8). Thus the hymn forms the new world. Ricoeur, in an important theological link, relates this movement to the problem of law and grace. He observes that the dislocation dislocates us from our project of "making a whole of our lives," "self-glorification," "salvation by works," and sets us into the world of grace.[76] For good reason, Dornisch concludes that "for Ricoeur, the restoration of meaning always moves toward kerygma."[77] The hymn sings good news.

V

We have appealed to three of Ricoeur's insights in understanding the Psalms.

1. Human experience, which is the name for what we are about, moves in a *painful* way from orientation to disorientation and in a *surprising* way from disorientation to reorientation.

2. We must utilize both hermeneutics, the *hermeneutic of suspicion*, which demystifies and disenchants, and the *hermeneutic of representation*, which resymbolizes and redescribes our life. (I have no term to describe a hermeneutic for the "psalms of orientation" reflecting stable life. Perhaps such a view is a "hermeneutic of convention.")

3. The use and function of this language are *not descriptive but evocative*. Its knowing use can receive new worlds for the community, given by God.

As concerns the practice of the Psalms in ancient Israel, it makes sense that the lament psalms are likely to be understood more personally or domestically,[78] whereas the hymns belong to the festival; for disorientation is much more intimate than reorientation. It likewise makes sense to follow Mowinckel in the notion that the festival of the cult is creative of the very experience it expresses, but now on the ground of the linkage between language and experience. The Psalms reflect the difficult way in which the old worlds are *relinquished* and new worlds are *embraced.*

Hopefully, in this admittedly subjective handling of ancient and contemporary pastoring, we have been as fair as possible to both. For contemporary pastoring, we hope to suggest that if we are attentive to the needs of people where they are, we have in the Psalms resources for helping persons both (1) live in the situation in which they in fact are, and (2) evoke in their lives new worlds of well-being that we know "dimly" (1 Cor 13:12) and in prospect.

The psalms of disorientation and reorientation are songs of scattering and gathering. The laments of Israel, like the hermeneutic of suspicion, are an act of dismantling and scattering for sheep without a shepherd (Ezek 34:5; Mark 6:34). The hymns and songs of thanksgiving in Israel, like the hermeneutic of symbolization, are an act of recollection, of consolidation, of new formations of wholeness when the shepherd is with the flock (Ps 23:1; John 10:10-11).[79]

As such, the Psalms are very much like our lives, which are seasons of scattering and gathering (Eccl 3:2-9).[80] We live always with the Lord of the exile, and all our songs to this Lord are from a strange land (Ps 137:4). This God has an intention of welfare and not of evil, to give a future and a hope. This God is the one who dares to say:

> I will . . . *gather* you from all the nations and all the places where I have *driven* you, says the LORD, and I will bring you back to the place from where I sent you into exile. (Jer 29:14)

> He who *scattered* Israel will *gather* him, and will keep him as a shepherd keeps his flock. (Jer 31:10)

> As a shepherd seeks out his flock when some of his sheep have been *scattered* abroad, so will I seek out my sheep; and I will *rescue*

them from all places where they have been scattered on a day of clouds and thick darkness. (Ezek 34:12)

The Psalms reflect the human experience of exile and homecoming. The reality of exile is partly a result of the stratagems of Babylon. But partly the matters of exile and homecoming happen in the practice of faithful imagination, in contexts of pastoring and liturgy. And in those contexts, where these poems live, songs of disorientation and reorientation do the work Fuchs characterizes as "world-destroying and world-forming."[81]

CHAPTER 2

God at Work in the Word: A Theology of Divine-Human Encounter in the Psalms

Harry P. Nasuti

One hardly needs to mount an argument for the theological significance of the book of Psalms. Throughout the history of both Judaism and Christianity, a host of major theologians have developed their understandings of God in conversation with this book, and these figures' writings on the Psalms are often counted among their most insightful works.[1] The Psalter has a similar prominence in the more narrow confines of modern biblical scholarship, and indeed the last few years have been especially fruitful in the appreciation of the theological richness of this book.

Despite this strong affirmation of the Psalms' significance, there is considerably less consensus as to the *nature* of this book's contribution to the theological enterprise. One common view is that the book of Psalms is important because it provides a condensed yet comprehensive version of theological themes found elsewhere in Scripture. So, for example, Athanasius likens this book to a garden containing all of what one finds elsewhere in the Bible, while Luther saw the Psalter as a "little Bible" for the same reason.[2] Along similar lines, modern biblical scholars have noted how the Psalter contains within itself all of Israel's theological traditions, from Exodus to David, creation to history to wisdom. Echoing Luther,

Hans-Joachim Kraus has argued that one could call the theology of the Psalms a "biblical theology in miniature."[3]

An alternative view is that the Psalter is not so much a useful compendium of what one finds elsewhere in the Bible as a work that speaks in a distinctive theological voice of its own. Those who hold such a view sometimes argue that the diverse individual psalms that make up the book have some sort of underlying thematic unity or at least a dominant emphasis. Such scholars often speak of the "center" or "heart" of the Psalter or have described what they see as its central metaphor. Some recent attempts along this line have seen God's justice or the destiny of the righteous as the thematic focus of the Psalter. Others have seen the description of God as king or refuge as its animating metaphor.[4]

It is also possible to see the distinctive contribution of the Psalter in the way that the individual psalms have been edited and shaped into a larger whole. Scholars who take this approach locate the point of the book of Psalms less in some common emphasis that underlies all (or most) of the psalms than in the relationship between these texts as they are now found in the Psalter. While such scholars may see most of the psalms as sharing some common image or theme (such as the reign of God), they would argue that the Psalter itself makes a more specific point by virtue of the way the individual psalms are situated in the context of the literary whole. So, for example, a number of recent scholars have seen the theological message of the book in its movement from Torah to praise or from lament to praise, as well as in a development from psalms concerned with human kingship to those emphasizing God as the one true king.[5]

While the approaches noted so far are obviously very different from each other, in one important respect they are actually similar. All of them primarily approach the book of Psalms as a source that provides information about God in a way similar to that found in the rest of the Bible. As in the case of the other biblical books, the interpreter's goal is to arrive at an accurate description of the picture that the text provides of God and God's relationship to Israel and humanity. The approaches outlined above may differ as to whether this picture is primarily to be found in the individual psalms or in the Psalter as a whole, but they agree that the theological method is one of description, that something is to be found *in* the text itself.

In this essay, I will not dispute the importance of arriving at a careful description of the theological contours of both the individual psalms and the Psalter as a whole. Instead, I will suggest that this description is only part of what constitutes the distinctive contribution of this biblical book. In doing so, I will argue that of at least equal importance for a theology of the Psalms is an understanding of the way these texts make available a relationship between God and the believing individuals and communities that have used them.

It is, of course, not unusual for scholarship on the Psalms to take note of their relational nature. The fact that many of these texts are intensely personal prayers addressed to God should ensure that any perceptive description of their theological themes will highlight their relational qualities. In addition, scholars that have argued for the central place of "righteousness" and "the righteous" in the Psalms have rightly emphasized the relational implications of those terms and the texts that contain them.[6]

The difference between such scholarship and what I suggest here is rooted in an attempt to appreciate the theological implications of these texts' continued use in the relational contexts of personal prayer and liturgy both throughout the history of Judaism and Christianity and at the present time. In this essay, I will argue that the sustained use of these texts in such a distinctive way implies a model of doing theology different from what has been discussed above, one in which the theologian's own stance before God (and that of his or her community) becomes an important part of any theological appropriation of these texts.

Theology, Theological Anthropology, and the Distinctive Contribution of the Psalms

One of the indications that the Psalms are inherently relational is the fact that one only rarely finds there a description of God in isolation from the world. It is instead God's relations with Israel, humanity, and the individual psalmist that constitute the theological focus of the Psalms.[7] Because of this, scholars have seen the Psalms not only as a source of theology in the strictest sense but also as the source of a theological anthropology that focuses on the theological implications of the way these texts depict humanity in relationship with God.

Thus, for Gerhard von Rad, it is in the Psalms "if anywhere" that we can "hope that the basic features of a theological doctrine of man will become clear—that is, that we may see *the* picture of man set over against the living God, and not merely a variant of the many pictures which man has made of himself."[8] It is, however, not simply a concern with the human side of the divine-human relationship that constitutes the distinctive theological contribution of the Psalms for von Rad. That concern is, after all, present throughout the Bible, from the speeches of the prophets to the narratives of the historical books. Rather, what is distinctive about the Psalms is that here the human side of the relationship is present in its own voice.

This is the deep insight of von Rad's well-known description of the Psalms as "Israel's answer."[9] This answer is "theologically a subject in itself" in that "in the course of her converse with Jahweh Israel did make further striking statements about herself over and above those general concepts of man which theologically do not amount to much." Indeed, "in this intercourse with Jahweh Israel was revealed to herself."[10]

Von Rad's analysis sheds considerable light on how the obviously human, first-person words of the Psalms could be seen as revelatory for ancient Israel. Nevertheless, there still remains the further question of how these texts continue to function as a theological resource for later generations of believers. Do they now function as a source of information about God and humanity in much the same way as the rest of the Bible, namely, as part of the historical (but still relevant) record of ancient Israel's theological insights? Or does the fact that these texts continue to be used as first-person

speech mean that they are not only part of ancient Israel's theological witness but also in some way part of an ongoing—and still
revelatory—conversation with God?

In some ways, this is the question behind Hans-Joachim Kraus's
wrestling with whether a theology of the Psalms is an objective or
a subjective enterprise. On the one hand, Kraus wants to affirm the
"objectivity of our theological work" by seeing a theology of the
Psalms not in terms of a "history of Israelite piety" but rather as a
description of the "testimony by which those who sing, pray, and
speak point beyond themselves, the 'kerygmatic intention' of their
praise and confession, their prayers and teachings." To this end, he
quotes von Rad's assertion that "the subject-matter which concerns
the theologian is, of course, not the spiritual and religious world
of Israel and the conditions of her soul in general, nor is it her
world of faith, all of which can only be reconstructed by means of
conclusions drawn from the document; instead it is simply Israel's
own explicit assertions about Jahweh . . . its specific kerygmatic
intention."[11]

On the other hand, Kraus also wants to argue that this is not
to say that in working toward a theology of the Psalms "we should
abandon the realm of the 'subjective' for that of the 'objective.'"
Along these lines, Kraus cites Karl Barth's observation that "the
object and theme of theology and the content . . . is neither a subjective element nor an objective element in isolation. This is to say, it
is neither an isolated human nor an isolated God, but God and man
in their divinely established and effective encounter, the dealings of
God with the Christian and of the Christian with God." Because
of this, Kraus argues that in dealing with the Psalms "we cannot
maintain a distance, and cannot eliminate the existential relationship to this event."[12]

Again, Kraus quotes Barth to argue that theology is "a task that
not only begins with prayer and is accompanied by it, but one that
is to be carried out appropriately and characteristically in the act of
prayer." Kraus then elaborates that "only in our encounter with the
Psalms are we brought to the basic recognition that anything said

of God in the third person is inauthentic; explicitly or implicitly, God can be thought of and spoken of truly and authentically only in the second person of direct address."[13]

What then is the relationship between the objective and the subjective in Kraus's thought? For Kraus, "The theology of the Psalms involves a constant effort to remain true to its subject matter—God and Israel, God and the person in Israel, in their encounter and fellowship, established by God and brought to realization by God. It involves God's dealings with the person and the person's dealings with God."[14]

There is much to consider here. One may begin by noting that Kraus quotes von Rad in his affirmation of the objective nature of the enterprise, while he quotes Barth in his affirmation of its subjective aspects. In this regard, it is perhaps significant that his citation of von Rad is not from the latter's treatment of the Psalms but from his more general thoughts on Old Testament theology. Certainly, Kraus's own *Theology of the Psalms* contains a considerable amount of work that would fall under the category of the "objective" treatment of these texts, with considerable attention to the names and descriptions used to depict God in the Psalms.

It is less clear how Kraus's work preserves the subjective aspect appropriate to these texts. Kraus would agree with von Rad that Israel's own experience is central to any theology of the Psalms. He would also undoubtedly argue that the divine-human relationship described in the Psalms is fundamental to the way contemporary Christians should understand their own relationship with God. The latter seems to be part of what Kraus has in mind when he says that a theology of the Psalms "involves a constant effort to remain true to its subject matter."

In all of this, Kraus clearly takes seriously the nature of the Psalms as Israel's prayer, the definitive first-person record of Israel's encounter with its God. The remaining question is whether Kraus's view of the Psalms does full justice to these texts' continued use as first-person speech in Jewish and Christian prayer and worship. It is, after all, precisely this continued use that would seem to lead most naturally to the Barthian view of theology as something done in the second person.[15]

What needs to be considered is the possibility that the Psalms may not only be subjective in the sense that they provide access to ancient Israel's first-person response to God. Rather, they may be seen as even more authentically subjective in that they have provided and continue to provide later generations of believing subjects with their own first-person response to a God who continues to call forth—and make possible—that response.[16] To use Martin Buber's well-known terminology, the Psalms do more than make available a description of Israel's past I-Thou relationship with its God. They also mediate a present I-Thou relationship between contemporary believers and their God.[17]

With this in mind, it may not be entirely sufficient to speak, as Kraus does, of an "encounter with the Psalms." One should also speak of an encounter with God that takes place through the use of the Psalms. The one who does theology on the basis of such an encounter does so not simply as an objective analyst of an important text but also as a praying subject in the company of a larger community of worship and shared life. It is the continued power of the Psalms' first-person speech that constitutes these texts' distinctive theological contribution.

The Distinctive Theological Contribution of the Psalms: Insights from Recent Scholarly Approaches to the Cult

For those familiar with the history of modern biblical scholarship, the discussion in the previous section may well call to mind certain developments in how that scholarship has approached the somewhat controversial topic of the cult. Throughout the last century, most scholars have usually (at least) downplayed the cult as a positive source for theological reflection. Such scholars often tended to value history or prophecy as the locus of Israel's authentic theological contribution while seeing the cult as either derivative of or in opposition to that contribution. Very often, the dynamics of the cult were seen to run counter to a proper faithful relationship with God.

Such a view of the cult is reflected even in the work of Hermann Gunkel, who, despite his attention to the institutional settings of psalm genres, still distinguished most of the canonical psalms from cult settings both chronologically and religiously.[18] Claus Westermann was even less interested in the institutional setting of the Psalms, concentrating instead on their larger theological "setting" in the relationship between God and Israel.[19] Kraus saw cult and ritual as "mechanisms for making adaptations and producing results, in a world of autonomous experiences" as opposed to "standing before God." For Kraus, such mechanisms belong to the sphere of "religion," which he saw as the "primordial threat to man."[20]

The major exception to this perspective is, of course, Sigmund Mowinckel, who saw the cult in much more positive terms, as a sphere of sacramental power capable of shaping its participants in important ways.[21] On the one hand, subsequent biblical scholarship has generally not accepted Mowinckel's historical arguments about the actual shape of ancient Israelite worship.[22] On the other hand, Mowinckel's more foundational insights about the nature of cult have recently become important for a number of Psalms scholars.

Mowinckel's key insight was that the cult is "effective and reality generating . . . a sacrament."[23] Rather than simply expressing what already exists (either in the participants' minds or the world), the cult enables its participants to have a present experience of God. It also anticipates and helps to bring about an alternative future. What Mowinckel affirmed for the cult, more recent scholars have affirmed for the Psalms, not only in terms of their role in ancient Israel, but also for their continuing use by believing individuals and communities.

Of these scholars, Walter Brueggemann is the perhaps the most explicit in his affirmation of the value of Mowinckel for understanding the "world-making" and "transformative" aspects of the Psalms.[24] However, other scholars, both ancient and modern, have also emphasized the ability of the Psalms to bring about something not present before their use. Athanasius speaks of the special power of these texts to "affect," "mold," and even "constrain" the person who prays them.[25] He also sees this power as related to the fact that the Psalms continue to be first-person speech, becoming the prayers of those who use them.[26] The modern scholar James Luther Mays sees a similar connection between the Psalms' distinctive power and their continuing role as first-person speech. Mays sees the Psalms as "means of grace," which have the power to transform those who use them into "the 'I' and the 'we' whose praise and prayers and meditations the Psalms express."[27]

As I have noted elsewhere, such a "sacramental" or "transformative" view of the Psalms not only fits well with Mowinckel's views of the cult; it also is very much in keeping with certain contemporary views of the way that language works, including speech-act theory and the work of such scholars as Paul Ricouer and Ludwig Wittgenstein.[28] It also fits well with those theologians who see Scripture in general as having sacramental or transformative power, even though these scholars do not always work out the special dynamics of the Psalms.[29]

It should be noted that both the negative and the positive views of the cult envision some type of encounter (or at least an attempted encounter) between worshipers and their God. On the one hand, those who are more skeptical of the cult see it as an illegitimate human attempt to manipulate God. On the other hand, those who see the cult in a more positive light tend to emphasize the way that through it God can have an effect on humanity. In the case of the Psalms, those scholars who have taken a sacramental or a transformative view have noted the way that God uses the Psalms to shape believers into the type of person that God wants them to be.

The Distinctive Contribution of the Psalms: Insights from Metaphorical Theology

One of the most fruitful approaches to biblical theology in recent years has been that which examines the metaphors for God present in the Bible. Not surprisingly, a number of scholars have taken this approach in their attempt to write a theology of the Psalms.[30] In view of the insightfulness of such studies, it is worth considering how this concern for metaphor intersects with an approach that takes seriously the Psalms' continued use in individual prayer and communal worship.

Because the Psalms continue to function as first-person speech, they do not simply provide a description of God but also help to bring about a particular relationship with God. In the case of metaphor, this means that the Psalms enable the praying individual not just to understand a divine metaphor but also to participate in that metaphor by assuming a particular role. The result is that the metaphors present in a particular psalm help to put the individual in a position to encounter God as God truly is and not as one would like God to be.

Recent Psalms scholars have taken note of this distinctive power of metaphor with reference to God as king. So, for example, Mays has argued that this is the "root metaphor" and the "center of the Psalms."[31] For Mays, the Psalms are the "liturgy of the Kingdom of God." Their continued use as first-person speech in the devotional and liturgical life of Judaism and Christianity has put individuals in those communities in "the role of servants of the Lord God."[32]

While not as pervasive as the metaphor of God as king, other metaphors (such as shepherd, judge, savior, refuge, rock) contribute to the larger theological portrait of God in the book of Psalms. This is obviously not the place for a comprehensive discussion of all of these metaphors and the way that they have a formative effect on those who use them in the act of prayer.[33] Nevertheless, given the argument of this essay, it might be useful to look briefly at two metaphors somewhat less often highlighted by Psalms scholars in their theologies of the Psalms, namely, the images of God as healer and as teacher.

While these metaphors are clearly rooted in the Psalms themselves, one could understand their being less prominent in theologies that attempt to describe either the God of the ancient psalmists or even, at least in the case of the metaphor of healer, the God of the Psalter's final redactors. It is, however, noteworthy that these images seem to take on some importance among later Jewish and Christian interpreters of the Psalms, precisely because those interpreters were at least in part constructing their theologies based on the actual experience of God that the Psalms made possible for them.

God as Healer

The metaphor of God as healer in the Psalms is rooted in both specific requests for God to heal[34] and in more explicit affirmations about God's role as healer.[35] This metaphor allows for a certain theological characterization of God, one that highlights both God's graciousness and God's power over creation. Such a description is often made explicit in the psalms that use this metaphor.[36]

Along with describing God in this way, these psalms also characterize those who pray them as in need of healing. On the one hand, form critics have often located these psalms in situations related to serious illness, and these texts have continued to be used to express the concerns of those in similar situations. On the other hand, throughout the history of their use, these psalms have never been limited to literal physical illness. Rather, they have also been seen as prayers for healing from other kinds of external distress,[37] as well as from the more spiritual "sickness" of sin.[38] Such wider connections have their basis in the Psalms themselves, but they are taken much further by later interpreters.[39]

This interest in sickness and healing leads to a view of God as the divine physician, a description that both the Jewish and Christian traditions have developed at great length and in many directions. While this description of God as healer may be rooted in psalms that specifically speak of healing, it can also be found in these traditions' interpretations of other psalms. So, for example, even though Psalm 51 is clearly more concerned with sin than with sickness,[40] both Jewish and Christian treatments of that text often use medical imagery that describes an encounter between the praying individual in need of healing and a God who is able and willing to heal.[41]

Of particular importance in this understanding of God as the divine physician is the role of the psalm itself. For a number of interpreters, the praying of the Psalms is necessary and effective medicine, the means by which one returns to spiritual health.[42] In such a way, the psalm itself, and indeed the Psalms as a whole, comes to be seen as the means by which the divine physician is at work healing those who pray them.[43] In other words, it is through the psalm that the individual is brought to an encounter with the compassionate God who has the power to heal.

God as Teacher

Alongside the petition for God to heal, the Psalms are full of requests that God teach and statements that God has taught or will teach both the psalmist and others.[44] Certain psalms, of course, are explicitly devoted to the praise of God's Torah or instruction (so Pss 1, 19, 119). However, the connection between God and teaching is not restricted to such psalms or to psalms that have been seen to have explicit wisdom concerns. Rather, this concern for God's teaching is to be found throughout the Psalter, and its significance is emphasized by the prominence of the introductory Psalm 1, which helps to highlight this theme in the rest of the book.[45]

As was the case with the language of healing, these references to divine instruction do more than describe God as someone who has the authority to teach and who has imparted important instruction. They also characterize the speaker as someone who is both appreciative of and committed to God's teaching. Even more, a number of the psalms envision God's continued instruction and the need for the speaker's ongoing openness to learning what God will teach. In some cases, the speaker also takes on an additional commitment to teach others what God has taught.[46]

Once again, later Jewish and Christian interpreters have picked up on this imagery and developed it further in their own approach to the Psalms. Particularly striking in the Jewish tradition are a number of midrashim in which David is seen to be a model student of Torah as well as someone who inspires others to be the same. Notable in some of these is the way in which David plays his harp and psaltery to awaken others to Torah study.[47] In such a way, David and the Psalms awaken Israel to the need to attend to God's teaching.[48]

Christian interpreters also stress the role of God as teacher in the Psalms, as may be seen from Calvin's comment that "he who wants to make progress in the school of God needs the psalms."[49] As in the midrashic examples, Calvin sees David as someone who is taught by God and who goes on to teach others, both by his example and by what he has made available in the Psalms.[50] Using both teaching and healing metaphors, Calvin notes that those who peruse the Psalms are "most effectually awakened to a sense of their maladies and, at the same time, are instructed in seeking remedies for their cure."[51]

Concluding Observations on Metaphor and the Psalms

One may conclude this section by noting a significant character-istic that the metaphors of healing and teaching share, especially as they have been developed in the Jewish and Christian tradi-tions. As was true in Mowinckel's full-bodied view of cult, an individual's participation in these metaphors is both a present and a future reality. On the one hand, these psalms enable those who pray them to assume a present stance (patient, student) with respect to God and so to have an experience of God in keeping with the metaphors of divine physician and teacher. On the other hand, this experience leads the praying individual to look forward to God's future actions with regard to him or her and the world. As in the case of cult, participation in the Psalms' metaphors is both a present experience and an anticipation of something that will take place in the future, at least in part because of what has transpired in the praying of the psalm.

The metaphors of the Psalms are particularly effective because they are part of these texts' first-person speech. As such, praying individuals are involved in the poetics of these texts in an unusu-ally intimate and transformative way. Also contributing to the effectiveness of such metaphors is the fact that even a single psalm will often contain a number of different divine metaphors. The result is a more complex encounter with a multifaceted and often surprising God.

Encountering God in Absence and Presence

In this essay, I have argued that one of the most distinctive aspects of the Psalms is their ability to mediate a divine-human encounter through their continued use as first-person speech by praying individuals. By enabling the praying individual to assume the correct stance before God, these psalms help to make available an experience of God. It is, however, obvious that the first-person speech of many psalms is marked not by any easy encounter with God but by a deep sense of God's absence. This has not gone unnoticed. A number of scholars have made questions of absence and presence a significant part of their theological understanding of the Psalms. The work of such scholars is, on the whole, extremely perceptive, and its consideration will help to illustrate the distinctive theological contribution of the Psalms.

Von Rad's analysis of the lament psalms in his *Old Testament Theology* can form the touchstone for this discussion. Quoting Barth, von Rad notes that "all true knowledge of God begins with the knowledge of his hiddenness."[52] The situation found in the laments, that "God had hidden himself so completely from the despairing man who had trusted in his mercy," was "Israel's hardest burden."[53] Yet von Rad also asserts that because such an individual is "cast upon Jahweh alone," that individual is led to both faith and "the most sublime spiritual communion with God."[54]

A similar dynamic of absence and presence can be found in other scholars' analyses of the Psalms. This is especially true of Samuel Terrien, who treats the Psalms in his work *The Elusive Presence: The Heart of Biblical Theology*. Like von Rad, Terrien sees a sense of God's absence as something that ultimately leads to faith. Indeed, he argues that absence and want lead to an "experience" of God, "as one who knows water by thirst."[55] For him, it was God's "very hiding which disclosed to [the psalmists] not only the meaning of their existence but also the intrinsic quality of divinity."[56]

Jerome Creach offers a similar argument.[57] For Creach, the righteous keenly feel the apparent absence of God in a world where the righteous suffer and the wicked prosper. This leads the righteous to prayer, trust, and right conduct, all of which contribute to an awareness of being in God's presence.[58] According to Creach, this dynamic is built into the structure of the Psalter itself, as may be seen in the concerns of its introduction, Psalms 1–2. These psalms highlight the importance of David, Zion, and Torah, "three sources of and witnesses to divine presence and protection."[59]

All of these authors see a hard-won affirmation of God's presence as that which sustains the righteous even in times of God's apparent absence. This affirmation of a continuing relationship with God is clearly to be found in a number of the texts that these authors treat. Nevertheless, it is important to note that in many of these texts the problem of God's absence—especially as indicated by the concrete suffering of the one lamenting—still remains. While the praying individual may have come to believe in and value his or her ongoing relationship with God in spite of God's apparent absence, it would not be true to say that the latter situation has become less significant, either for the individual concerned or for the theology of the Psalms.

Indeed, other Psalms scholars have voiced important cautions about moving too quickly to a more purely spiritual view of the relationship. For example, Westermann has argued that the importance of the lament lies in the fact it gives voice to suffering and brings it before God: "This is its function: to appeal to God's compassion. All the multifarious forms of human affliction, oppression, anxiety, pain, and peril are given voice in the lament, and thus it becomes an appeal to the only court that can alter their plight."[60] Westermann does see the lament as a way of "clinging to God," even in such an extreme case as that of Job. However, this is "a clinging to God against God" rather than a relationship that is in any way an answer to the suffering that prompted the lament in the first place. For Westermann, "Doubt about God, even the kind of despair that can no longer understand God, receives in the lament a language that binds it to God, even as it accuses him."[61]

Brueggemann similarly insists that one should not move too quickly past the concrete situations of human suffering that underlie the lament. He argues that issues of suffering and justice are central in the Psalms and that "Israel is not interested in spirituality or communion with God that tries to deny or obscure the important issue of theodicy."[62] In his view, God assumes different roles in the conversations about theodicy that one finds in the Psalms, at times being the "harbinger of new justice to be established" and at other times being the one who is challenged "in the disorientation."[63]

It is worth considering the theological significance of this view of the lament for how one understands the God that one encounters in the continued use of these texts. A number of the above scholars have argued that these psalms represent the psalmists' attempts to maintain a relationship to a God felt to be absent. However, it is also important to note that in their subsequent usage these psalms that have their origins in an experience of God's absence become themselves the means by which God becomes present.

For generations of Jews and Christians, such human prayers have been understood to be divinely inspired, sanctioned, and even prescribed as part of both the canon and traditional liturgical practice. As the Word of God given to believers for their own normative prayer, the lamenting—and even the challenging—of God's absence at the heart of these texts is not just a natural expression of a human feeling of abandonment. Such an act is also God's own insistence that believers should refuse to accept the present situation as final, even if that means taking the audacious step of demanding that God act like the God who is confessed elsewhere in the Psalter. In such a way, these texts may be seen as part of the divine—no less than the human—attempt to maintain the divine-human relationship.

Both Westermann and Brueggemann have noted the reluctance of at least some believers to challenge God in this way. Westermann has described the minimizing of the "complaint against God" in postexilic Judaism and especially in Western Christianity.[64] For him, the neglect of this aspect of the lament does not do justice to God's own engagement with human suffering that one sees elsewhere in Scripture and especially to the fact that the New Testament places Psalm 22 on the lips of the crucified Jesus.[65] Brueggemann has also noted the reluctance to use the lament psalms and argued that this is indeed a "costly loss" that results in a false picture of God.[66] One might, of course, add that if such reluctance exists, it does so in serious tension with these psalms' presence in canon and liturgy, both of which support the view that they are clearly prayers that God wants to be prayed.

The original psalmists were painfully aware of God's absence in their lives and in the world at large, and through the Psalms they gave voice to both that pain and their trust in God's continued faithfulness. Should others also experience God's absence in their lives, these texts may be used to express and give form to their experience as well as to enable them to embrace a similar faithful relationship with God. If, however, such texts do not describe these individuals' lives, these psalms constitute God's own insistence that those who pray them be aware of and protest God's absence in the world of other, not-so-well-placed individuals. In such a way, those who pray these psalms truly encounter a living God who interacts with them in different ways depending on their situation in life and their standing before God.

The divine-human encounters mediated by the continued use of the lament psalms have significant theological implications. These psalms reveal a God who is somehow present even in the deepest experience of God's absence. Such a God insists on the recognition of—and the protest against—suffering, even at the cost of calling God to account. In the encounters mediated by these psalms, one meets a God vulnerable and open to serious challenge, even if (as in the book of Job) God does not provide a definitive answer to the individual's complaint.[67] In the long run, one also meets a God who is capable of inspiring trust, even in the face of such continuing questions.

The Encounter with God in the Psalms: Divine and Human Perspectives

In this essay I have tried to make the case that the continued use of the Psalms as first-person prayer implies a distinctive way of doing theology, one rooted in a present encounter between God and those who pray these texts. Along the way, I have taken note of a number of the implications of this approach for how one might construct a theology of the Psalms. Before going on to summarize these implications, it might be useful to look further at some of the specific ways this encounter has been seen to work, both in the interpretive tradition and in modern scholarship.

It is possible to consider this issue from two perspectives. First of all, one may look at it theologically, in terms of how one conceives of the divine action in this encounter. As I have already observed, taking note of this encounter envisions that God not only in some way inspires the human author by calling forth the original response of a certain psalm; God also continues to be active in the praying of the psalm by subsequent individuals, working through the psalm to shape that person in important ways.

Interpreters and theologians describe this active role of God in various ways. One may first of all note the common description of the Psalms in Christian circles as "means of grace," a gift that God gives and through which God works to enhance the life of faith.[68] Also important in this tradition is the argument that the Holy Spirit is active in the praying of the Psalms as much as in their original creation.[69] A particularly graphic image of the role of the Spirit may be found in the work of Gregory of Nyssa, who sees God's work in the Psalter as that of a sculptor "chiseling us to his divine likeness."[70]

A somewhat different approach sees the praying of the Psalms in terms of corporate personality. Along such lines, Christians have often seen Jesus as praying the Psalms on behalf of the church with particular effectiveness.[71] In a somewhat similar way, the Jewish tradition sees David's special relationship with God as that which makes praying the Psalms effective and appropriate for all generations of Israel.[72]

All of these approaches share the conviction that the effectiveness of the Psalms is not something entirely dependent on the praying individual's own power and worth before God. Rather, at least as important is God's initiative and graciousness that underlies the praying of the Psalms. In these texts, God is at work from within to bridge the distance between divine and human. This fits well with the traditional view that the liturgy is ultimately "God's work," something that God does and that has an effect on those who participate.[73]

From the human perspective, one may first describe those elements that facilitate the Psalms' effect on those who use them and then go on to spell out the implications of such elements for theology (and theological anthropology). As has already been seen in the previous section on metaphor, one factor in the Psalms' effectiveness is surely the fact that as poetic texts they have an aesthetic effect that goes beyond the simple imparting of information. In addition to metaphor, the presence of such poetic devices as sound and structure (including but not limited to parallelism) involves the reader in ways that are not always fully translatable into cognitive terms. This aesthetic effect is augmented when the Psalms are set to music.

Also contributing to the ability of the Psalms to affect believers is their frequent use in communal liturgical contexts. In human terms, such contexts may be seen as a primary means by which individuals are socialized into enduring systems of belief and practice. In a more theological perspective, these may be seen as opportunities of grace through which God works to transform participants into the individuals God wants them to be.

Even more, the use of particular psalms in specific liturgical contexts certainly facilitates their appropriation by individuals, even if it does not completely determine that appropriation. So, for example, the fact that Psalms 113–18 constitute the Hallel, sung at Jewish festivals throughout the year, provides an important background for their individual use at other times. The same is true of psalms associated with Christian feasts, such as Psalm 22 or 116.

This liturgical use points to another element that enables and shapes the effect of the Psalms on those who pray them; namely, the fact that a number of them are associated with characters whose stories are found elsewhere in the canon. So, for example, Jewish tradition associates Psalm 22 with Esther at Purim, while Christian tradition links that psalm with Jesus during Holy Week. Such characters are often at the center of particular liturgical settings, and they provide believers with models for identification and imitation. By stipulating the praying of the Psalms associated with these figures, the liturgy helps bring about the transformation of those who use them.

Even when there is no specific liturgical tie, the presence of a literary connection between psalm and character allows for a transformative dynamic in the use of the Psalms. For example, the close connection between David and the Psalms in both Jewish and Christian traditions can lead those who pray these texts to identify with David and to imitate his relationship with God. In such a way, both Jewish and Christian uses of Psalm 51 have been influenced by their association with David and his sinfulness in the case of Bathsheba and Uriah. These traditions often urge the faithful to imitate David in his repentance.[74] The praying of Psalm 51 is one means by which such an imitation is actualized and the necessary repentance is brought about.

To summarize, one may point to the Psalms' aesthetic elements, their use in communal liturgical settings, and their association with specific foundational events and characters as significant elements in their continued use and effectiveness. One may briefly take note of the implications of these features for the theological anthropology of the Psalms before moving on to more general theological conclusions.

These elements point in two different directions. On the one hand, the aesthetic elements may possibly be taken as an indication of a general human ability to be spiritually moved and morally changed by art and beauty, as well as of the need for any theological anthropology to incorporate more than a cognitive view of humanity's relationship with God. On the other hand, the association with a specific community, with its particular historical memories and significant individuals, would appear to echo the observations of those like von Rad who see any theological anthropology based on the Psalms as one that goes beyond observations about humanity in general. This will be discussed further in the section that follows.

Conclusions: A Theology of Divine-Human Encounter in the Psalms

What then are the theological implications of the types of divine-human encounters mediated by the Psalms in their continued use? First of all, such encounters point to a God who has taken and continues to take the initiative in dealing with humanity. Far from being the object of human manipulation, the God of the Psalms is one who stubbornly remains a subject, even while remaining open to serious challenge. This divine subject continues to reach out to humanity in a personal way, with specific intentionality for each person, pursuing goals that the psalm itself brings closer to reality in the way God interacts with the person praying it.

Second, the divine-human encounter of the Psalms takes place in the specific context of God's relationship with Israel, as that relationship is mediated in ongoing communities by both liturgy and the wider canon of Scripture. The God encountered by the believer in the Psalms is one whose goal for the individual is part of a larger divine plan for Israel and, through Israel, for all of humanity. Despite the fact that many (though certainly not all) of the psalms seem to lack a wider historical focus, their liturgical and literary ties to Israel's history mean that the person who prays them is not simply an isolated individual or even a generic representative of all humanity. Rather, that person is related to a specific history rooted in Israel and carried on by the faithful communities of Judaism and Christianity throughout the ages.

The fact of this history also means that the God encountered in the use of the Psalms is not a stranger to those who pray these texts—and also that a theology of the Psalms can never be entirely separated from a theology of the wider canon and its interpretative traditions. Nevertheless, because the encounter that takes place through the use of the Psalms is at the same time a present reality, the God encountered there is very much a "living" God who interacts with those praying these texts in different ways depending on their life situations and their relationships with God. A theology of the Psalms that takes account of this present encounter must always be acutely aware of the cautions of those theologians who see the "second person of divine address" as the only authentic way of speaking about God.

With such cautions in mind, one may perhaps conclude by suggesting that the distinctive theological contribution of the Psalms lies precisely in the eschatological urgency of how God is at work in them. As a number of scholars have noted, the Psalms' persistent expectation of God's future actions gives them a decidedly eschatological orientation.[75] It is, however, important to add that this attitude of future expectation is rooted in a present divine-human encounter made possible by the Psalms themselves. Any theology based on the Psalms takes place in the give-and-take of an ongoing relationship. Like many relationships, that which manifests itself in the continued use of the Psalms has a significant history and a future that will defy expectations. The center of this relationship, however, lies in an often troubled but intimate present, in which each participant addresses the other in the most honest and searching terms. As a primary site of this present encounter, the Psalms continue to be one of the most effective ways that both God and humanity work to ensure that their relationship continues.

CHAPTER 3

The Destiny of the Righteous
and the Theology of the Psalms

Jerome F. D. Creach

Throughout much of the modern period, the study of the book of Psalms has tended to highlight the Psalter's rich diversity and thus its lack of unity. But the question eventually arises, Is there anything in the Psalms that allows them to be read all together? Approaches to the Psalter that emphasize genre and *Sitz im Leben* tend to limit the understanding of unity to features of a particular type of psalm or to the common function of psalms as Israel's response to salvation.[1] But do the Psalms themselves contain any common feature or theme that permits them to be read as a book? Is it possible to discern any theological dimension expressed in or assumed by all the psalms?[2]

In this essay, I will propose that such an organizing rubric may be found in the Psalter's concern for the life and destiny of the righteous.[3] To identify this topic as an entrée into the Psalter is to identify a subject that is largely ignored in contemporary faith communities. Indeed, the word *righteous* along with the related word *wicked* have all but fallen out of the vocabulary of religious speech today. Perhaps for that reason the problem of the righteous and their future has been generally overlooked in discussions of the theology of the Psalter. Nevertheless, this theme is pervasive in the book of Psalms and, as Gerhard von Rad said, "There is absolutely no concept in the Old Testament with so central a significance for all the relationships of human life as that of" righteousness.[4] I will suggest therefore that the concern for the destiny of the righteous has potential to serve as the primary theological context for other subjects that have received more attention in recent years, subjects such as the reign of God and the divine attempt to establish justice and peace.[5]

The words *righteous* and *wicked* are often associated with narrow, legalistic, and condemnatory expressions of faith. But such associations, of course, are based on misunderstandings of this language and what it signifies. The term *ṣaddîq* ("righteous") in the Psalms refers to those who depend on God for protection (34:7), those who plead to God for forgiveness (38:18), and those who worship God in humility (17:15).[6] Such persons are not morally pure; rather, they call on and align themselves with the righteousness of God (5:9). But perhaps most importantly, this word identifies a group of people powerless before an oppressive enemy and therefore seeking God's mercy and justice (143). These characteristics of the righteous suggest the term *ṣaddîq* is virtually synonymous with the terms *ʿānî* ("poor"), *dal* ("oppressed"), and *ʾebyôn* ("needy"). Psalms 9 and 10, to cite but one example, place these words alongside each other in extended descriptions of those who are at the mercy of the wicked (Ps 10:7-18; see also Amos 2:6-8). The fact that the righteous rely on God in such circumstances suggests further they should be identified by the terms *yāšār* ("upright"; 73:1) and *ʿebed* ("servant"; 90:13, 16). As James Luther Mays says, the righteous relate to God as a servant to a king who is their lord.[7]

The stance of the righteous before God sets them apart from the wicked. While the righteous praise God (33:1) and pray to God when in trouble (37:39-40), the wicked "flatter themselves," as Ps 36:3 puts it; "greedy for gain," the wicked "curse and renounce the LORD" (10:3). This contrast between the righteous and the wicked is ubiquitous in the Psalms and appears in a variety of expressions. Thus, I am proposing that these two radically different ways of life constitute the basis of the theology of the Psalter, that virtually every theological problem or conviction in the book may be traced to the character of the righteous and to their uncertain future in relation to the wicked. Before examining this proposal further, however, it would seem helpful to justify the selection of this topic as the starting point for the theology of the Psalms more extensively.

The Destiny of the Righteous as Central Subject: Supportive Evidence

The notion that the destiny of the righteous is a central theological concern in the Psalter is supported first and foremost by the sheer frequency of the language in the book. Anyone who reads through the book of Psalms is surely struck by the attention to the righteous and how life will turn out for them. The Psalter begins with a psalm that sets forth the life of the righteous over against the wicked (1:1-3) and then declares what the end will be like for the two groups: the wicked will be swept away in judgment, while the righteous are kept in God's care (vv. 4-6). In the psalms that follow, the concern for the righteous does not diminish. The term *ṣaddîq* and its plural form, *ṣaddîqîm*, occur 52 times in the Psalms. Only Proverbs uses the term more often (66 times). The word "upright" (*yāšār*) appears 25 times, more often in the Psalms than any other book. In all, the terms noted above that describe the righteous appear 125 times in the Psalter. Furthermore, the term *rāšāʿ* and its plural, *rĕšāʿîm*, which signify those who oppress and persecute the righteous, appear 82 times in the Psalter, far more frequently than any other book of the Hebrew Bible.

The impressive number of occurrences of these terms alone makes it hard to deny the crucial role the righteous play in the Psalter. But the interest in the righteous and their future is even more pervasive than this vocabulary indicates. It should be noted that the righteous are only identified as such by third-person references; they do not call themselves righteous. The righteous appear again and again in the Psalter in the voices of those who pray. Or put another way, the prayers in the Psalter that call out to God for help are the prayers of those the Psalms call righteous. When this is recognized, it might well be concluded that the destiny of the righteous is the primary subject of the Psalms.[8]

The Destiny of the Righteous and the Shape of the Psalter

The central role of the righteous in the Psalms is also suggested by and made more understandable through the literary structure or "shape" of the Psalter.[9] Although a comprehensive examination of the shape of the Psalter is not possible here, a brief discussion of portions of the book suffices to make the point.

The righteous and their future is the primary subject of Psalms 1 and 2, psalms that form a dual introduction to the Psalter. Although these two works are quite different in tone and content, they are united by an interest in the two ways one can choose in life—the way of the righteous and the way of the wicked—and by the future of the two groups. Psalm 1 is thoroughly dominated by this subject. Psalm 1:1 begins with the declaration, "Happy are those who do not follow the advice of the wicked." The psalm then depicts the righteous as those who meditate on and delight in torah (1:2) and whose future is secure because the righteous are grounded in divine instruction (1:3). Psalm 1 ends by contrasting the destinies of the righteous and the wicked: "The LORD watches over the way of the righteous, but the way of the wicked will perish" (1:6).

Psalm 2 does not use the terms "righteous" and "wicked," but it addresses the subject implicitly by presenting two paths in life that portray these categories, especially when Psalm 2 is read with Psalm 1. Scholars have often noted that Psalms 1 and 2 share vocabulary that links them to each other and perhaps even indicates that Psalm 2 was edited to bring it in line thematically with Psalm 1.[10] The lexemes shared between the two psalms in nearly every case serve to contrast those who go the way of God and those who oppose that way. For example, while the righteous in

Psalm 1 "meditate" on the Torah of the Lord (1:2), the nations in Psalm 2 "meditate" on plans to thwart the work of God (2:1; in both cases using the Hebrew *hāgâ*); in Psalm 1 the "way" (*derek*) of the righteous is observed and rewarded by the Lord, but the way of the wicked will "perish" (*ʾābad*; 1:6). Similarly, in Psalm 2 those who oppose the Lord and the Lord's anointed will "perish in the way" (*tōʾbdû derek*; 2:12). Perhaps the most obvious link between the two psalms is the word *ʾašrê* ("happy"), which creates an envelope around Psalms 1 and 2 (1:1; 2:12). This term characterizes the righteous as those who enjoy God's favor (and are thus "happy" or "fortunate"), and it sets them apart from the wicked, who know only God's wrath.[11]

The final statement in Psalm 2 summarizes the character and destiny of the righteous, even as it warns the rebellious nations of the way they should go: "Happy are all who take refuge in him" (v. 12). This has a larger theological and editorial significance in Psalm 2. It does enhance the connection between Psalms 1 and 2, but it also points forward to the many descriptions of the righteous as those who "take refuge" in the Lord in the rest of the Psalter.[12] Hence, as Psalms 1 and 2 invite the reader into the book, they present the character of the righteous as an example to follow and the destiny of the righteous as something to ponder.[13]

The language Psalm 2 shares with Psalm 1 gives a particular cast to the wicked. Namely, it places the wicked under the rubric of "enemies."[14] Hence, the two introductory psalms suggest that the identity of the righteous and the wicked in the Psalter is both individual and corporate.[15] The righteous are both unnamed individuals who suffer and Israel suffering under its enemies. The wicked, likewise, are both those who oppress the poor and the nations that oppress Israel. As the following examples from Psalms 3, 41, and 72 will show, this dual identity of the righteous and their plight is borne out in the Psalter's portrait of the person of David.

Psalm 3 is set "when he [David] fled from his son Absalom." The most outstanding feature of the portrait of David in Psalm 3 is not his power or influence. Rather, the picture is of one who cries out to God when beset by enemies. As Mays says, David's name in Psalm 3 and elsewhere "does not so much claim the psalms as the voice of a king as it identifies him, in the psalms that are claimed for David, with the lowly."[16] The psalm opens with recognition of being overwhelmed by adversaries ("O LORD, how many are my foes!" v. 2) and records the taunt of the enemy ("There is no help for you in God"; v. 3). The word "many" appears three times in the first two verses to denote the dire circumstances ("how many are my foes" [*rabbû*], v. 2a; "many are rising against me" [*rabbîm*], v. 2b; "many are saying" [*rabbîm*], v. 3). The consensus of those who oppose the anointed, as it were, is that "there is no help for you in God" (v. 3). And yet David confesses, contrary to his foes' claim that God cannot help him, that "you, O LORD, are a shield around me" (v. 4).

David's dependence on God is evident. In the face of enemies rising (*qāmîm*) against him (v. 2b), he calls on God to "rise up" (*qûmâ*) and deliver (v. 8a). Matching the threefold reference to the "many" foes, Psalm 3 uses the word *yĕšûʿātâ* ("deliverance," "salvation," or "help") three times to confess that God alone can deliver (vv. 3, 8a, 9). The sequence of the three appearances of the term drives home this point. The adversaries taunt that there is no "help" in God (v. 3); David cries for God to "help" or "deliver" (v. 8a); then at the close of the psalm he confesses that "deliverance" belongs to God (v. 9). Psalm 3 thus presents David as representative of those who confess to being "poor and needy" (40:18).[17] In other words, he is one of the righteous who suffers at the hands of the wicked.

The concern for the destiny of the righteous also appears prominently in psalms that end books 1 and 2 of the Psalter.[18] The psalm at the end of book 1 emphasizes the character and destiny of the righteous in ways much like Psalms 1 and 2. Psalm 41 begins with the word "happy," the same term at the beginning of Psalm 1 and at the end of Psalm 2. Therefore, as McCann has observed, all of book 1 is framed by an interest in the human situation, particularly in what characterizes human happiness.[19] Psalm 41 focuses on the concern for the righteous specifically in the attention it pays to those who "consider the poor" (v. 2). Hence, book 1 ends just as the Psalter began, with an expression of faith that God watches over the righteous and ensures their destiny.

Psalm 41, like the psalms at the beginning of the Psalter, also seems to identify the king as both the model of righteousness and as the defender of the righteous. Although the person identified here is not called "king" explicitly, that identification makes sense in light of the characterization of the person as one who considers the poor.[20] If Psalm 41 indeed has the king in mind, he is presented here like the anointed in Psalm 2: he is the earthly expression of divine justice and protection.

Psalm 72 concludes book 2 with a prayer for the monarch, focusing on the ruler's care for the righteous, much like Psalm 41 concludes book 1. Psalm 72 introduces the king as one who is to "judge your people with righteousness, and your poor [ʿānî] with justice" (v. 2). Verses 12-14 most explicitly present the monarch's supreme concern for the poor: he "delivers the needy" (v. 12), "has pity on the weak and needy," and "saves the lives of the needy" (v. 13). Verse 14 includes perhaps the strongest statement of the king's care for the righteous. It says he redeems (yigʾal) their lives "from oppression and violence." He "has pity" on them (v. 13) and "precious is their blood in his sight" (v. 14). In other words, the righteous are not a distant concern of the king's administration; indeed, their needs are his first concern. Moreover, the fact that the king's actions on behalf of the righteous are characterized as "redemption" (v. 14) suggests the king identifies with the righteous as with a near kinsman (Ruth 3:13; 4:4, 6).[21]

So, books 1 and 2 both end with psalms that portray the ruler as one whose primary concern is the destiny of the righteous. But the final psalms in books 1 and 2 are not the only sign of concern for the righteous. Indeed, both books end with a cluster of psalms that highlight this concern and perhaps even show signs of intentional shaping around it. At the end of book 2, three other psalms address the righteous and their future. Psalm 69 is a prayer for deliverance uttered by one of the righteous. The one who prays petitions God for the wicked to "be blotted out of the book of the living; let them not be enrolled among the righteous" (v. 29). Then the psalmist confesses to being "lowly" (ʿānî; v. 30) and in need of divine protection. The one who prays promises to offer true praise; that is, praise greater than mere sacrifice (vv. 31–32). The brief psalm that follows concludes with the declaration, "But I am poor and needy; hasten to me, O God! You are my help and my deliverer; O Lord, do not delay!" (70:6). Psalm 71 continues this confession before the final psalm in book 2, which, as already noted, presents the character of the king who defends the righteous.

The end of book 1, as well as displaying parallels to the beginning of the book, contains language and theological concerns remarkably similar to the psalms at the end of book 2. In fact, the words of Psalm 70 simply appear as Ps 40:14–18. Because of the psalm doublet, the psalmist confesses to being "poor and needy" at a penultimate place in book 1 just as in book 2 (Pss 40:18; 70:6). The focus on the righteous at the end of books 1 and 2, however, is more extensive than the mere repetition of Psalm 70. In the first half of Psalm 40, the psalmist speaks of a scroll that records the character of the righteous: "Then I said, 'Here I am; in the scroll of the book it is written concerning me that my delight is to do the will of my God; indeed, your instruction is in my inward parts" (my translation; vv. 7–8). The "scroll of the book" here likely refers to a document in which the names of the righteous are recorded so they can be duly rewarded.[22] It has a close parallel in Ps 69:29, in which the psalmist wishes for the wicked to be blotted out of God's book. Furthermore, Ps 40:7 contrasts the psalmist's delight in God with burnt offering and sin offering in way very similar to Ps 69:32. Hence, the repetition of Psalm 70 as Ps 40:14–18 generates a set of parallels, all of which draw attention to the piety and plight of the righteous. Since Psalm 70 was likely borrowed to form the present ending of Psalm 40, it is therefore possible to argue that the end of books 1 and 2 were shaped to enhance the reader's view of the character and destiny of the righteous.[23] Even if the endings of books

1 and 2 were not formed for this purpose editorially, the common focus on the righteous and the wicked in these two portions of the Psalter is nevertheless unmistakable.

This brief sketch centering on Psalms 1 and 2 and the first two major junctures in the book suggests the first half of the Psalter is dominated by the concern for the destiny of the righteous. Whatever other subjects may appear in the Psalms, they may be identified within and understood as part of this larger concern for the righteous and their future.

One may observe similar emphases in subsequent divisions of the Psalter. The following observations represent a sample of the prominence of the concern for the righteous in rest of the Psalms: Psalms 107 and 145, which frame book 5, highlight God's goodness to the righteous, for whom God extends *ḥesed* ("steadfast love").[24] In book 5, the Lord's steadfast love to the righteous is perhaps the central subject. The term appears six times in Psalm 107 (vv. 1, 8, 15, 21, 31, 43); it appears in the first and last verses of the psalm and in a fourfold refrain that structures the poem (vv. 8, 15, 21, 31). *Ḥesed* is also prominent in Psalm 145 in the declaration, "The LORD is gracious and merciful, slow to anger and abounding in steadfast love" (v. 8). Psalms 107 and 145 likewise declare God's care for the righteous and his certain provision for a secure future. Psalm 107 emphasizes throughout that God cares for those in distress (for example, v. 9 declares that he "satisfies the thirsty" and "fills the hungry"), and verses 41-42 put this in terms of the destiny of the righteous:

> But he raises up the needy out of distress,
> and makes their families like flocks.
> The upright see it and are glad;
> and all wickedness stops its mouth.

In a similar way, Psalm 145:19-20 states,

> He fulfills the desire of all who fear him;
> he also hears their cry, and saves them.

The LORD watches over all who love him,
   but all the wicked he will destroy.

Hence, book 5 begins and ends with promises that God will
make the righteous flourish and will bring the wicked to an end.
Moreover, before the five psalms that conclude the Psalter give way
to pure praise, they state again the concern for the righteous. Psalm
146:9 declares,

The LORD watches over the strangers;
   he upholds the orphans and the widow,
   but the way of the wicked he brings to ruin.

The Destiny of the Righteous and the Reign of God

Reading the Psalter in the way here proposed would seem to bring
order and coherence to many dimensions of the Psalms. For example, the psalmist's frequent protestation of innocence makes sense
as the cry of the righteous when accused by the wicked (Pss 7:4-6;
17:1). Psalms of imprecation are more accessible when read as the
cries of those who are helpless before forces opposed to God.

This organizing rubric also has potential to illuminate the
larger concept of the reign of God, which scholars have sometimes noted as an organizing subject in the Psalms. In a seminal
essay, James Luther Mays argues that the Hebrew sentence, *Yhwh
mālāk* ("The Lord reigns") is the central theological claim in the
Psalter and serves as its organizing center.[25] Mays is certainly right
that the understanding (1) of God as king and (2) of the world as
God's kingdom orders and explains the Psalter's claims about God
more than any other theological concept. In the Psalter, however,
concern for the destiny of the righteous provides the theological context for the claim that "the Lord reigns." This is apparent,
for example, in Psalm 5, which contains the first occurrence of
the label *melek* ("king") for God in the Psalter. Here the psalmist invokes God's kingship as part of a plea for deliverance from
the wicked. The psalmist calls on God with confidence that God's

just rule does not permit wickedness to prevail (v. 5) and that the Lord, as a beneficent monarch, spreads protection over the righteous (vv. 12-13).

Concerning the larger questions of the structure of the Psalter, the sentence *Yhwh mālāk* ("The Lord reigns") occurs most frequently in a portion of the Psalter that was edited to address the problem of the righteous and wicked on a large scale.[26] Book 4 (Pss 90–106) wrestles with the fact that the righteous people, Israel, have suffered defeat and exile and responds to that circumstance with the continued affirmation that "the LORD reigns" (Pss 93:1; 96:10; 97:1; 99:1; NRSV translates the sentence in each case, "the Lord is king").[27] In other words, the affirmation that "the Lord reigns" is offered in the midst of circumstances that would seem to indicate otherwise, circumstances centered on the situation of the righteous vis-à-vis the wicked.

Attention to the Psalter's concern for the destiny of the righteous also puts into perspective three other topics sometimes associated with the reign of God: the king, Mount Zion, and Torah. Each of these three subjects represents a tangible sign of God's sovereignty. They may be understood, in the organizing rubric proposed here, as the "embodied hope" of the righteous.[28]

1. We have already noted that David appears in the Psalter as both a righteous sufferer and as defender of the righteous. He suffers at the hands of the wicked and cries out to God for help (Psalm 3). But as the Lord's anointed (Ps 2:2), David is also the monarch who represents the heavenly king on earth. His main charge is to ensure justice for the "poor" (see Psalms 72; 101). Hence, the king, David—at least in his ideally presented role—is for the righteous a primary sign on earth that God's order, justice, and righteousness are at work for their sake.

2. Mount Zion, on which the earthly king is enthroned and from which God's reign is shown to the world, is the particular place on earth where the righteous experience God's presence and protection. Zion is thus the place the righteous long to be (Psalms 42–43). As Psalm 92 describes, on Zion, and in its temple,

The righteous flourish like the palm tree,
 and grow like a cedar in Lebanon.
They are planted in the house of the LORD;
 they flourish in the courts of our God. (Ps 92:13-14)

3. Torah is the source of life and blessing on which the righteous "meditate day and night" (Ps 1:2). As Ps 1:3 makes clear, the righteous are made secure, "like trees planted by streams of water" as a result of meditating on Torah.[29] Torah is the "polity of the reign of God," and, as such, it is the ultimate hope for the righteous.

Conclusion

To summarize the position: The book of Psalms is supremely concerned with the future of those it calls righteous. This concern permeates the Psalter in terms of frequency of appearance, and it appears in key elements of the book's structure as well. When the Psalter is read with the destiny of the righteous in mind, it brings order to other major subjects, such as the reign of God, the role of the human king, Mount Zion and its temple, and Torah.

In conclusion, it seems worth noting that at least one early Christian community seems to have read the Psalter with precisely this focus on the destiny of the righteous. According to Luke 23:47, at the death of Jesus the centurion beneath the cross "praised God and said, 'Truly this man was righteous'" (my translation). Here the centurion uses the Greek term (*dikaios*), which is equivalent to the Hebrew word *ṣaddîq*. Later, when Jesus explains to his disciples that his suffering, death, and resurrection were foretold "in the law of Moses, the prophets, and the psalms" (Luke 24:44), it is likely the suffering of the anointed in the Psalms that stands in the background of Jesus' reference to the Psalter. Indeed, in Acts 2, Peter appeals to the suffering of David in the Psalms and to God's vindication of David to explain the suffering and resurrection of Jesus (Acts 2:25-36).[30] In other words, the author of Luke-Acts paints a picture of Jesus as one who suffers like the righteous in the Psalms. Jesus' destiny—his resurrection and continued presence with God—is understood as patterned after the destiny of the righteous in the Psalter, particularly as the righteous are represented by the anointed of the Lord, David. It was largely because of this connection that the early church saw the book of Psalms as a work of theological gravity and that the Psalms continued for centuries to be read as an "abiding theological witness" to Jesus Christ.[31]

The Single Most Important Text in the Entire Bible: Toward a Theology of the Psalms

J. Clinton McCann Jr.

I imagine that if somehow one could manage to reach every person in the world who identified himself or herself as a Christian and could ask them the question, What is the most important text in the whole Bible? No one would answer, "Psalm 82," with one exception. But this exception is a major one! His name is John Dominic Crossan; and he is one of the most productive, well-known, and influential biblical scholars in the United States, and indeed the world. In his 1998 volume *The Birth of Christianity*, Crossan asserts that Psalm 82 is "the single most important text in the entire Christian Bible."[1]

Now, of course, given the circumstances I have just described—John Dominic Crossan's opinion over against that of the entire Christian world—one could reasonably conclude that Crossan, while he may be an expert and is certainly entitled to his own opinion, is simply wrong. Fair enough. But for the sake of this essay, I am going to invite you, the reader, to play along. Even if you think Crossan is wrong, suspend your better judgment for the moment, and give him the benefit of the doubt; and give me the benefit of the doubt, because I am going to argue that Crossan is right, or at least is on the right track.

I readily admit that my motives for agreeing with Crossan may not be entirely pure and unbiased. After all, I am an *Old* Testament scholar, and more specifically a Psalms scholar. So I think it is just great that John Dominic Crossan, a famous *New* Testament scholar, has concluded that the single most important text in the Bible is found in the *Old* Testament, and even better, in the book of Psalms! In any case, I am going to try to convince you, the reader, that Psalm 82 is the most important text in the whole Bible. If I cannot convince you of that (and I probably cannot), then I am going to try to convince you that Psalm 82 is at least, in the words of Frank-Lothar Hossfeld and Erich Zenger, "one of the most spectacular texts of the OT."[2] And if I cannot convince you of that, I want to try to demonstrate in any case that Psalm 82 is crucially important for understanding the Psalms and especially for beginning to move toward a theology of the book of Psalms.

The Singular Importance of Psalm 82

Let us return to Crossan for a moment in order to appreciate why he thinks Psalm 82 is the most important text in the entire Christian Bible. The following quotation contains Crossan's description of the content of Psalm 82 and how he interprets it. I have added in brackets a few verse citations that are not in the original:

> [Psalm 82] is, for me, more important than John 1:14, which speaks of the Word of God becoming flesh and living among us. Before celebrating that incarnation, we must address a prior question about the character of the divinity involved. And that short psalm best summarizes for me the character of the Jewish God as Lord of all the world. It imagines a mythological scene in which God sits among the gods and goddesses in divine council [v. 1]. Those pagan gods and goddesses are dethroned [vv. 6-7] not just because they are *pagan*, nor because they are *other*, nor because they are *competition*. They are dethroned for injustice, for divine malpractice, for transcendental malfeasance in office. They are rejected because they do not demand and effect justice among

the peoples of the earth. And that justice is spelled out as protecting the poor from the rich, protecting the systemically weak from the systemically powerful [vv. 2-4]. Such injustice creates darkness over the earth and shakes the very foundation of the world [v. 5].

. . . Psalm 82 tells us how we are to be judged by God *but also how God wants to be judged by us* [my emphasis]. Everything else that God says or does in Bible or life should be judged by that job description [vv. 3-4]. Is this or that the transcendental justice defined in Psalm 82 at work? Or is this or that just transcendental testosterone?[3]

Notice that, for Crossan, the issue is explicitly theological—that is, the issue is the essential character of the biblical God. And notice too, as Crossan suggests, that God's essential character is inextricably linked to justice, which is very specifically defined as protection of and provision for those whose lives are most threatened and vulnerable.

In the NRSV translation of Psalm 82, the English word "justice" shows up only once (v. 3); but the Hebrew root underlying this word shows up four times—once in each of verses 1-3 and again in verse 8. That is to say, justice is emphasized both by the sheer number of its occurrences—four times in eight verses—and by the fact that it appears in both verses 1 and 8, forming an envelope structure for the poem. Because certain gods in the ancient Near East were expected to protect orphans and widows and the poor, the warning to the gods in verses 3-4 seems like it would be a standard way of criticizing the gods, or at least someone else's gods. But according to Hossfeld and Zenger, verses 3-4 offer "a radical new accent" to the topic of the gods and the poor. They describe this radicalization in part as follows:

While in ancient Near Eastern texts the obligation to protect orphans, widows, and the dispossessed rested only on individual "law deities," our psalm makes this obligation of protection the crucial mark of the divinity of all deities, and thus the essential characteristic of divinity pure and simple.[4]

Thus, according to Psalm 82, what it means to be God—what characterizes divinity—is to protect and provide for the lives of the most threatened and the most vulnerable, not by offering charitable handouts but rather by what Hossfeld and Zenger call "comprehensive alteration in social and political conditions"[5]—in a word, *justice*, understood systemically as transformative opposition to "the hand" or "the power" of oppressors, named here by the repeated term "the wicked" (vv. 2, 4).

Given the criticism of the gods for their failure to enact justice, it is fitting that Psalm 82 concludes with the only poetic line in the form of a prayer (v. 8); and it is a prayer for justice on nothing short of a world-encompassing scale. The God who took a stand in verse 1 (and has not been mentioned by name since then) is directly addressed and implored to arise and to "establish justice" (my translation). By the way, the correspondence between verses 1 and 8 suggests the probability of an intentional chiastic arrangement of the entire psalm, as suggested by Lowell K. Handy,[6] with verses 2-4 corresponding to verses 6-7 (both sections being addressed to the gods). Such a structure means that verse 5 is the structural center of the poem, thus highlighting its devastating assessment of the failure of the gods and/or the wicked to do justice—that is, "all the foundations of the earth are shaken." In other words, the creation reverts to chaos.

Verse 5 is extraordinarily important and timely, and I will call attention to it again below when, in the conclusion of this essay, I offer one final reason that Psalm 82 is the most important text in the Bible. But let me build toward that conclusion by first attempting to demonstrate how Psalm 82 seems to function within the book of Psalms—that is, how it relates to other key aspects of and texts within the Psalter and thus how it serves to highlight crucial theological dimensions of the book.

Psalm 82, the Psalter's Theological Heart, and Its Messianic Orientation

Psalm 83 is the final psalm "of Asaph" in the Psalter (see Psalms 50, 73–83); and Hossfeld and Zenger suggest that the Asaphite collection concludes with an intentional arrangement of Psalms 79–83.[7] Psalms 79 and 80 are communal laments that describe the destruction of Jerusalem, the defilement of the temple (79:1), and the taunting of God's people by "the nations," including the question in 79:10, "Where is their God?" Recalling past deliverance from distress in the form of the exodus from Egypt, Psalm 81 looks to a time when "there shall be no strange god among you" (81:9). Our psalm, Psalm 82, explains why there shall be no strange gods— that is, God will dethrone them. Psalm 82 also provides a pointed answer to the question of 79:10: "Where is their God?" Well, in Psalm 82, *their* God is dethroning *your* gods. Now granted, this all sounds dangerously imperialistic (a point to which I shall return in a moment), but it is more understandable and more palatable on the part of a people who have heard their enemies say, "Come, let us wipe them out as a nation" (83:4). Psalm 83, the final psalm of Asaph, prays for what Psalm 82 has envisioned and described—that is, the removal of the threat by the nations due to the dethroning of their gods. Psalm 83 ends, like Psalm 82, affirming the universal sovereignty of God:

> Let them know that you alone, whose name is the LORD,
>   are the Most High over all the earth. (83:18)

As Konrad Schaefer observes of Psalm 82 (and it would apply also to Psalm 83), "The psalm ends on a universal note which will be played out in the latter part of the Psalter."[8] In addressing the crisis of exile and its aftermath by asserting God's universal claim on "all the nations" and "over all the earth," Psalms 82 and 83 anticipate at least book 4 of the Psalter (90–106), which includes a collection of "God-reigns" psalms (93, 95–99). According to Gerald Wilson, book 4 was shaped in response to book 3 (73–89), especially its conclusion, Psalm 89, which effectively articulates the crisis of exile by recounting the rejection of God's "anointed," the Judean king (see 89:38-51, a passage bounded by references to "your anointed"). More specifically, by announcing that God still reigns in the midst of the crisis, Psalms 93, 95–99 form the Psalter's "theological 'heart,'" according to Wilson—that is, God reigns.[9]

A brief analysis of Psalm 96, the first psalm in the core (96–99) of the God-reigns collection, will demonstrate how its content has been anticipated by Psalm 82. Because "all the nations belong to you [God]," as Psalm 82 affirms, Psalm 96 logically invites "all the earth" to praise God (96:1, 9), along with the "families of the peoples" (96:7). "The nations" and "all the peoples" need to be told about God's "glory" and God's "marvelous works" (96:3), because their gods "are idols" (96:4), a claim recalling the dethroning of the gods in Psalm 82. The proclamation "The Lord is king" is made "among the nations" (96:10) and is immediately followed by an announcement that specifically counters Ps 82:5. Whereas the reign of the gods meant that "all the foundations of the earth are shaken," God's reign means that "the world is firmly established; it shall never be moved" (96:10; "shaken" in 82:5 and "moved" in 96:10 translate the same Hebrew verb).

And why, according to Psalm 96, is the world stable and safe? Because—again like Psalm 82, answering the taunting question posed by the nations in Ps 79:10, "Where is their God?"—God "is coming to establish justice [on] the earth. / He will establish justice [in] the world with righteousness, / and [among] the peoples with his faithfulness" (96:13; my translation). According to Psalm 96, God will do what the gods failed to do—bring about justice and righteousness; indeed, on nothing short of a world-encompassing scale, as indicated by the creation-wide response in Ps 96:11-12 to God's coming, which is joyfully greeted by heavens and earth and sea and field and "all the trees of the forest." In short, Psalm 82, with its emphasis on God's world-encompassing claim and God's commitment to justice, connects clearly with Psalm 96 and the affirmation that forms the theological heart of the book of Psalms— God reigns.

At the same time that Psalm 82 anticipates the Psalter's theological heart, it also connects very clearly with another major feature of the book of Psalms that has theological significance—the book's messianic orientation, evidenced most clearly by the appearance of royal psalms (that is, psalms about the Judean king known as the "anointed one," the Hebrew of which is ordinarily transliterated as *messiah*) at crucial junctures in the book—Psalm 2, as part of the Psalter's paired introduction; Psalm 72, at the end of book 2 (42–72); and Psalm 89, at the end of book 3.

Now, it may be entirely coincidental, but notice that Psalm 82 is in the vicinity of both Psalms 72 and 89—not exactly equidistant between the two, but close. In any case, a reader who is at all conversant with the book of Psalms, even when he or she is not reading the book sequentially, cannot miss the fact that what the gods were told in Ps 82:3-4 that they should have been doing—justice and righteousness, measured by protection of and provision for the most threatened and vulnerable—is precisely what the Judean king is entrusted with in Psalm 72 (see especially 72:1-7, 12-14; see "delivers" in 72:12 and "deliver" in 82:4).

This fact, along with the fact that Psalm 89 relates the rejection or dethroning of the Judean king, gives Ps 82:6-7 a particular significance, especially the claim that the "gods . . . shall . . . fall like any prince." For, by the end of book 3, God has dethroned not only the gods (82) but also the Judean king (89), who is known elsewhere as God's own "son" (2:7; 2 Sam 7:14). All this should undercut any tendency or temptation to appropriate Psalm 82 imperialistically. God plays no favorites. God shows no partiality, not even to God's own *messiah*, God's own "son." When the Judean kings fail to do justice, they too, just like the gods in Psalm 82, "fall like any prince." If God shows any partiality, it is only to justice, defined as the systemic creation of conditions that make life possible for all, especially for the ones whose lives may be the most threatened and vulnerable.

The connection of Psalm 82 both to the Psalter's theological heart and to its messianic orientation reinforces the portrayal in Psalm 82 and the whole Psalter of God as essentially, characteristically a God of world-encompassing justice. For this reason, Crossan has at least a very credible case when he asserts that Psalm 82 is "the single most important text in the entire Christian Bible." But there is more. Not only does Psalm 82 connect to the Psalter's theological

heart and its messianic orientation; it also connects with the introduction and conclusion to the book of Psalms.

Psalm 82, the Psalter's Introduction, and Its Conclusion

Although very few translations of Psalm 1 contain the word "justice," the Hebrew word *mišpāṭ* does occur in Ps 1:5, where it is usually rendered "judgment." But rather than a typical translation of
Ps 1:5a, such as the NRSV's "Therefore the wicked will not stand
in the judgment," it is possible to translate Ps 1:5a, "Therefore the
wicked will not stand when justice is done," or perhaps, "Therefore
the wicked will not stand up for justice." In any case, for the purposes of this essay, it is crucial to note that the key word in Psalm
82, "justice," also occurs in Psalm 1, thus connecting Psalm 82 lit-
erarily and conceptually with Psalm 1. Both are concerned to point
out that the wicked do not conform to the justice that God wills
for the world.

When this connection is recognized, the effect is to suggest to
the reader of Psalm 1 a particular understanding of the repeated
word *tôrâ* in Ps 1:2. Not only should the word *tôrâ* not be translated
as "law" (see the NRSV and many other major translations) but also
the more accurate translation—"teaching" or "instruction"—should
be understood to have a particular content—namely, justice (cf.
94:12-15; 119:132-136). In other words, Psalm 1 commends constant attention to what God teaches, or we might say, to what God
characteristically wills; and this is justice. At this point, of course,
Psalm 1 is performing quite well its function of introducing the
Psalter, since it is anticipating not only Psalm 82, but also Psalms
93, 95–99, which, as suggested above, form the Psalter's theological
heart, portraying God as "coming to establish justice (on) the earth"
(96:13; 98:9).

Psalm 82's highlighting of justice as the crucial criterion of
divinity also connects it to the conclusion of the Psalter. The concluding collection of the Psalter consists of Psalms 146–150, all of

which begin and end with "Praise the LORD!" Not surprisingly, the first psalm in this concluding collection explicitly recalls Psalm 1 by way of its mention of "happy" (146:5; see 1:1), as well as its description of what happens to "the way of the wicked" (compare 146:9 and 1:6). Then too, Ps 146:10 also recalls the Psalter's theological heart when it affirms that "the LORD will reign forever." Along the way, Ps 146:7, which perhaps not coincidentally is the central poetic line of the psalm, affirms that God "executes justice for the oppressed." Again, the effect is to recall the theological heart of the Psalter, along with Psalm 82 and its highlighting of justice.

Psalm 149 also recalls the theological heart of the Psalter when it mentions "a new song" (149:1; see 96:1; 98:1), and when it calls God "King" (v. 2). Like Psalm 146 also, Psalm 149 recalls the introduction of the Psalter. In particular, the description in Psalm 2 of how the earthly king will rule over the nations (2:8-9) is echoed in Ps 149:7-8. The crucial difference is that Psalm 149 assigns the rule over the nations not to the earthly king but instead to "the faithful" (vv. 2, 5; see v. 9), and this dominion over the nations is explicitly described as "doing among them the justice decreed" (v. 9; my translation). Again, the effect is to recall both Psalms 1 and 2, as well as the theological heart of the Psalter, and Psalm 82. In addition, it seems that the conclusion of the Psalter has taken into account the disappearance of the monarchy (see Psalm 89), which, like the gods in Ps 82:7, has taken a "fall like any prince." In short, it is easy to hear resonances of the message of Psalm 82 as the Psalter reaches it conclusion.

Toward a Theology of the Psalms: Psalm 82, Praise, and Prayer

The cumulative effect of all of the above is impressive. As it turns out, Psalm 82 has literary and conceptual connections with major aspects and key texts of the Psalter—with the introductory Psalm 1 by way of the term "justice"; with the introductory Psalm 2 and the Psalter's messianic orientation (see 72 and 89, the concluding psalms of books 2 and 3); with the theological heart of the Psalter by way of the mutual emphasis on justice; and with the conclusion of the Psalter, both by way of the emphasis on justice again and by way of the apparent recognition in Psalm 149 that the monarchy has fallen, thus recalling Psalm 89, which documents the fall, and Psalm 82, which provides an explanation for the fall—namely, the failure to do the justice that God wills (and that God had entrusted to the kings, according to 72).

In the case of the latter two—that is, the connections among Psalm 82, the Psalter's theological heart, and its conclusion—the effect is to closely associate justice and praise. The pivotal position of Psalms 93, 95–99, along with the prominence of Psalms 146–150 as the conclusion of the Psalter, strongly suggest the conclusion that praise, whenever and wherever it occurs throughout the book of Psalms, should be heard both as an affirmation of God's reign and as an expression of commitment to God's world-encompassing will—in a word, justice. Thus Paul Westermeyer is surely on the right track when he reaches the following conclusion:

> Anybody who knows the psalms at all knows that . . . they are saturated with justice. . . . Justice is on every page of the Psalter . . . . Justice is sung throughout the psalms. Justice and song lead back and forth to one another, and the whole Psalter with all its concerns for justice leads to the song of praise in Psalm 150 toward which the whole cosmos is moving. The telos of praise to God contains justice within it as part of its very essence.[10]

And, of course, no single psalm so highlights the importance of justice for understanding God and God's purposes for the world as does Psalm 82. This is why Crossan identifies it as "the single most important text in the entire Christian Bible." And even if one concludes that this is something of an exaggeration, one must at least admit with Hossfeld and Zenger that Psalm 82 is "one of the most spectacular texts of the OT." And as I have tried to demonstrate in this essay, the content of Psalm 82, along with its connections to key texts and aspects of the book of Psalms, makes it crucially important for understanding the Psalter and for moving toward a theology of the Psalms.

Given the clear connection between justice and praise, given the proclamation in the songs of praise at the heart of the Psalter that the sovereign God is "coming to establish justice (on) the earth," and given that the book of Psalms in Hebrew is called "Praises," one might reasonably expect the Psalter to be an extended chorus of continuous and uninterrupted praise. But it is not. Indeed, beyond the introductory Psalms 1 and 2, the first psalm is an urgent prayer for help by a psalmist who is roundly assailed by enemies who tell the psalmist not to look to God for help (see 3:1-2). Constant opposition turns out to be the normal situation of the psalmists who pray what are commonly known as laments, complaints, or protests; and these prayers are actually the majority type in the Psalter.

The omnipresence of enemies in the Psalms (note that already in the introductory psalms, 1 and 2, God and those who look to God are opposed) has to be one of the most important theological data in the book, especially given the Psalter's vigorous proclamation of God's reign and its affirmation of the fundamental importance of God's will for justice in the world. What the pervasiveness of the enemies represents is that God's sovereignty does not take the form of sheer force. In short, God's will is regularly *not* done, and the result is the experience of persistent *injustice* on the part of those who pray the psalms. Why? The apparent answer is that for the sake of genuine relationship with humankind—that is, for love's sake—God has given humankind genuine freedom and the ability to respond.

The implications of this answer are profound. First, God's sovereignty is exercised ultimately as love, not force. Thus, as we move toward a theology of the Psalms, this means that, if there is a word in the Psalter that is as important as the word "justice," it is the word *ḥesed*, which the NIV often translates as "unfailing love" and the NRSV regularly translates as "steadfast love." The parameters of this essay do not permit a developed discussion of *ḥesed* in the

Psalms, but see the essay in this volume by Rolf Jacobson.[11] Second, the persistent injustice documented by the voice of prayer in the Psalms is an invitation to those who honor God's sovereign claim to enact the justice that God wills in and for the world. Thus, the Psalter presents a missional challenge that will be considered briefly in the conclusion to this essay.

Conclusion: Psalm 82 and Contemporary Life

In his discussion of the Psalms and their contribution to Old Testament theology, William Bellinger cites Ronald Clements, who suggests "that theology is not theology unless it has to do with contemporary life."[12] I think Clements is absolutely right; and so, in conclusion, let us return to Psalm 82 to consider one more reason that it may be at least one of the most important texts in the entire Bible—that is, the way in which it "has to do with contemporary life." In this regard, the structurally central verse 5 is of central importance. It reads as follows:

> They ["the gods" and/or "the wicked"] have neither knowledge
>> nor understanding,
>> they walk around in darkness;
>> all the foundations of the earth are shaken.

Although framed in the worldview of the ancient Near East, this assessment of reality is strikingly, startlingly, and chillingly contemporary. It is not hard to identify ways in which the foundations are shaking, ways in which the future of the earth is threatened—terrorism; growing extremes of wealth and poverty that mean thirty thousand children die every day of hunger-related causes; the AIDS pandemic, especially on the continent of Africa, that to date has created over 12 million orphaned children (recall "the orphan" mentioned in 82:3); a disturbingly fragile global economy; environmental distress, including the alarmingly high and unprecedented rates of disappearance of plant and animal species; and the growing evidence of what is called, somewhat euphemistically, climate change.

Even as the foundations are shaking, however, the fact is that the large majority of North Americans have benefited and continue to benefit from a global socioeconomic system that consigns millions, if not billions, of people to poverty. For this reason, John Goldingay, in his recently published commentary on the Psalms, concludes: "Psalm 82 therefore stands as one of the most *worrying* texts in the OT."[13] In the final analysis, I submit that Psalm 82 is so very important precisely because it is so worrying. Perhaps it will be worrisome enough to unsettle those of us who look to the Psalms as, in any sense, authoritative—worrisome enough to rouse us out of our comfortable complacency, so that we might take a stand with the God who vehemently opposes systemic injustice, so that we might take a stand with the God who claims not only our lives but the lives of "all the nations," and who wills the establishment of justice for us all, beginning with "the lowly and the destitute" (82:3).

CHAPTER 5

The Theology of the Imprecatory Psalms

Nancy L. deClaissé-Walford

A number of psalms in the Psalter are classified as "Imprecatory Psalms": Psalms 12, 58, 69, 83, 94, 109, 129, and 137.[1] Many other passages contain imprecatory language, including 17:13; 31:17; 35:4; 59:11-13; 69:22-28; 70:2-3; 139:19-22.[2] The words of the psalm singers ring harsh and shrill as they invoke God's wrath on their foes.

> Let his days be few;
>> let another take his position.
> Let his children become orphans,
>> and his wives widows.
> Let his children continuously roam about and beg;
>> let them offer entreaties from their desolate ruins.
> Let a lender lay a snare for all that belongs to him,
>> and let strangers treat his possessions with contempt.
>>> (109:8-11; my translation)

The imprecatory words of the Psalter call on God to take vengeance on other nations (137) and other individuals (109) who have harmed the psalmists in some way, those who have deprived the psalmists of freedom or have sought to destroy them physically, mentally, or spiritually. J. Carl Laney, in a 1981 article titled "A Fresh Look at the Imprecatory Psalms," defines "imprecation" as "an invocation of judgment, calamity, or curse uttered against one's enemies, or the enemies of God."[3] The words are sometimes spoken to God:

> Let them vanish like water that runs away;
>> like grass let them be trodden down and wither.
> Let them be like the snail that dissolves into slime;
>> like the untimely birth that never sees the sun. (58:7-8)

And the words are sometimes spoken to the oppressors:

> O daughter of Babylon, the one destroyed,
>> content will be the one who repays you
>> for your doings, that which you have done to us.
> Content will be the one who seizes and dashes
>> your suckling children against the rock. (137:8-9; my
>> translation)

How might we understand and interpret such words? How do they inform our understanding of God and God's relationship with humanity?

The Imprecatory Psalms in Their Canonical Context

A distinctive feature of the book of Psalms that sets it apart from other books in the Old Testament/Hebrew Bible is that it contains the words of humanity spoken to God rather than the words of God spoken to humanity (i.e., the prophets); words narrating the relationship between God and humanity (i.e., the ancestral and exodus stories in Genesis and Exodus); or words of instruction from God to humanity (i.e., Leviticus and Deuteronomy). Thus, might we be permitted to dismiss the imprecatory language of the Psalms as that of humanity and having little to do with the nature of God?

Throughout the years, scholars have presented mixed views of the imprecatory psalms. Some choose to contrast the violent and vengeful God of the Old Testament with the loving and forgiving God of the New Testament, thus rendering a discontinuity between Judaism and Christianity.

Artur Weiser, in his 1962 commentary that appeared in English in the Old Testament Library series, states in regard to Psalm 58:

> The psalm . . . shows the undisguised gloating and the cruel vindictiveness of an intolerant religious fanaticism; it is one of those dangerous poisonous blossoms which are liable to grow even on the tree of religious knowledge and clearly shows the limits set to the Old Testament religion.[4]

Hans-Joachim Kraus, in his commentary that appeared in the Continental Commentary series, writes of Psalm 137:

> The Christian community—in situations of oppression and sadness—will take up the lament of Israel; but only with reservations and critical deliberation will it be able to agree with the tenor of vv. 7-9 (Happy shall they be who pay you back what you have done to us!!).[5]

And Edwin McNeill Poteat, in the 1955 edition of *The Interpreter's Bible*, says of Psalm 83:

> This psalm is an unedifying and tedious catalogue of bloody violence. . . . These factors are largely responsible for the consensus that regards this psalm as one of the least religious of all the poems in the Psalter.[6]

There is no way to soften the words or alter the sentiments expressed in the words of the imprecatory psalms. Each is a heartfelt song sung to God, asking for God's justice to be meted out in the face of absolute despair and hopelessness. Each is a song of revenge sung on behalf of the victims of cruelty, despair, and destruction.

And so we return to the question. Ought we to dismiss such language to the periphery of the Psalter, to a few compositions in this otherwise praise-filled book? Ought we to dismiss such language to the periphery of our biblical text? Two observations argue against such a conclusion.

First, those communities of faith that shaped the texts into the canons of Scripture known as the Hebrew Bible or as the Christian Old Testament incorporated the book of Psalms (which includes the imprecatory psalms) into their canons.[7] In addition, the Septuagint Psalter includes the imprecatory psalms (all of them), as do the various Psalters discovered among the Dead Sea Scrolls.[8] While many of the psalms—including some, perhaps all, of the imprecatory psalms—were originally oral in nature, composed by individuals or the community as addresses *to* God, they were transformed by their inclusion in the canon from words *of* the faithful *to* God to words *from* and *about* God *to* the faithful. They are no longer the utterances of a particular community of faith to its God; they have became words about God for all communities of faith, across all times and all spaces, to their God.

By the very act of accepting the imprecatory psalms as a part of their canons of "Scripture," the Jewish rabbis and the Christian church leaders acknowledged the importance and value of these psalms for their overall understanding of the character and nature of the relationship between the God of the biblical text and the people who choose to worship that God. That is, communities of faith must have found value and insight into the character of their God in these texts, or they would not have preserved the texts for subsequent communities of faith. James A. Sanders writes in his 1980 essay, "Canonical Context and Canonical Criticism":

> There has been a relationship between tradition, written and oral, and community, a constant, ongoing dialogue, a historical memory passed on from generation to generation, in which the specific relationship between canon and community resided.[9]

Sanders goes on to say that communities find value in stories and texts when those texts provide answers to two basic existential questions: Who are we? and, What are we to do?[10] The ancient

Israelites repeatedly asked these questions of, and found answers to them in, their traditions—the stories and texts they passed on from generation to generation, which became authoritative for the life of the people.

Thus, we cannot summarily dismiss the imprecatory psalms and banish them to the periphery of the canon.[11] They are an integral part of the words of the psalmists, rendered by their inclusion in the canon as the words of God and embraced by millennia of the faithful as part of Scripture.

Second, imprecatory words are not confined to the book of Psalms; they occur in various places in the text of the Old Testament. Numbers 10:35 tells us that Moses spoke words of imprecation each time the ark of the covenant set out during the wilderness journey:

> Arise, O LORD, let your enemies be scattered,
> and your foes flee before you.

Deborah sings in Judges 5:

> So perish all your enemies, O LORD,
> But may your friends be like the sun as it rises in its might.
> (v. 31)

In Jer 18:19-20, the prophet implores God to take vengeance on his oppressors:

> Give their children over to famine;
> hurl them out to the power of the sword,
> let their wives become childless and widowed.
> May their men meet death by pestilence,
> their youths be slain by the sword in battle. (v. 21)

The author of Lamentations writes of those who participated in the destruction of Jerusalem:

> Pay them back for their deeds, O LORD,
> according to the work of their hands!

> Give them anguish of heart;
>> your curse be on them!
> Pursue them in anger and destroy them
>> from under the LORD's heavens. (3:64-66)

The writers of the New Testament both quote from the imprecatory psalms and provide their own words of imprecation against enemies. In Acts 1, Peter quotes from Pss 69:25 and 109:8:

> For it is written in the book of Psalms,
> "Let his homestead become desolate,
>> and let there be no one to live in it";
> and
>> "Let another take his position of overseer." (v. 20)

Matthew 10 tells us that Jesus sent out the disciples with specific instructions:

> If anyone will not welcome you or listen to your words, shake off the dust from your feet as you leave that house or town. Truly I tell you, it will be more tolerable for the land of Sodom and Gomorrah on the day of judgment than for that town. (vv. 14-15)

Paul says in 1 Corinthians:

> Let anyone be accursed who has no love for the Lord. (16:22)

And in Galatians:

> But even if we or an angel from heaven should proclaim to you a gospel contrary to what we proclaimed to you, let that one be accursed! (1:8)

Imprecatory words are found throughout the biblical text, not just in the words of the psalmists. Thus, they cannot be dismissed to the periphery of the canon or be excluded from our "canon within a canon." They must be wrestled with and appropriated into our understanding of God and humanity's relationship with God.[12]

Asking God to act in vengeance on behalf of a community or an individual is not an easy thing, though, to appropriate into twenty-first-century Christianity. We think of church, and most especially the worship experience, as a place and time where we are uplifted and where we give praise to God for God's good abundance to us. We listen to the organ prelude; the choir sings a song of gathering for the community; the minister invokes the presence of God; and the gathered community raises its voice in song to celebrate the sacred hour of gathering. Quite a production. In that sacred place and time, we are transformed and moved beyond the realm of the everyday, the realm of our usual being.

But what about those times when the world cannot be checked at the door of the church? What if the world intrudes, like a persistent, unwelcome visitor—ringing the doorbell over and over, knocking urgently on the door, peeking in through the windows—even though we try to ignore it? And what if that world is screaming in dissonance with the world our churches attempt to create in the worship event? What if the sentiments of the troubling psalms are all-consuming in our community of faith? What *if* a church member has been gang raped, fallen victim to a scam, been abused by a nursing home caregiver, been cheated out of their pension, lost a child to a drunk driver, been betrayed by a trusted friend? What *if* the people of your church are victims of hate crimes or are targeted for profiling in your neighborhood? What about the abject poverty and starvation brought about by corrupt governments throughout the world? What should be the response of the church?

Should we read, study, pray, and preach the imprecatory psalms and the vengeance-filled words of so many of the psalms? What can they tell us about the God we worship? What can they tell us about our response to the God we worship? For—and this is perhaps the hardest part of the imprecatory psalms to reconcile—the imprecatory psalms are outcries against violence that demand just such violence by God on behalf of the psalm singers.[13] These psalms ask for, indeed they demand, violence as an answer to violence. How do we, how can we reconcile such dissonance?

The Imprecatory Psalms
in Their Relational Context

Erich Zenger, in *A God of Vengeance? Understanding the Psalms of Divine Wrath*, tells a story of the prioress of a Carmelite convent in Dachau, Germany—an important stop for pilgrims who travel the paths of the Nazi annihilation of the Jewish people. In 1965, the nuns were given permission to "pray the Office" (the daily prayers of the church) in the vernacular rather than in Latin. After a trial period of reciting the Psalms in German, the prioress wrote:

> However, this vernacular prayer, which had become necessary and requisite for the sake of the tourists, also brought with it serious problems with our recitation of prayer in choir, because of the so-called imprecatory or vengeance psalms, and the cursing passages in a number of the psalms. We were soon tempted to return to Latin, for no matter how much the vernacular brought home to us the riches of the psalms, the Latin had at least covered up the weaknesses of the psalms as prayer. In the immediate vicinity of the concentration camp, we felt ourselves unable to say out loud psalms that spoke of a punishing, angry God and of the destruction of enemies. . . . Our prayer should be such that it can encourage people to reconciliation, forgiveness, and love.

In the end, the prioress chose to eliminate the imprecatory psalms from the public observance of the Liturgy of the Hours.[14]

Ought we, along with the prioress of Dachau, eliminate these psalms from our "liturgy"? A trip through the Revised Common Lectionary reveals some interesting insights. While most of the so-called psalms of vengeance are not included in the lectionary (Pss 12, 58, 83, 94, 109, and 129 are not), a few are, such as Psalm 79:1-9. And included in the reading from Psalm 79 are the words:

> Pour out your anger on the nations
>   that do not know you,

and on the kingdoms
>   that do not call on your name.
For they have devoured Jacob
>   and laid waste his habitation. (vv. 6-7)

Psalm 137—all of it—is also included, as are a number of passages that the Prioress of Dachau labeled "cursing passages." Thus, we cannot summarily eliminate these psalms from our liturgies. We must find a way to include them in our own canons within canons and to find within them insight into the nature of God. A look at four characteristics of the imprecatory psalms may be helpful in this endeavor.

First, the book of Psalms, not just the imprecatory psalms, is filled with references to "the enemy" and "the oppressor." Erich Zenger maintains, "The life of the people of Israel appears over-whelmingly to be a daily struggle, an ongoing battle against ene-mies."[15] The people who pray the psalms feel themselves surrounded, threatened, and engaged in battle by a gigantic army of oppres-sors; they feel like animals pursued by hunters and trappers; or they see themselves surrounded and attacked by rapacious wild beasts, trampling bulls, or poisonous snakes. Othmar Keel lists ninety-four words used in the Psalter to describe the psalmists' enemies.[16]

But, the "enemies," "foes," and "oppressors" in the Psalter are rarely named specifically. The references are general, leaving the readers or hearers to "fill in the gap" of identity, so to speak:

Psalm 7:6:   "O LORD, lift yourself up against the fury of my enemies."

Psalm 58:6:   "O God, break the teeth in their mouths; tear out the fangs of the young lions, O LORD!"

Psalm 129:   "May all who hate Zion be put to shame."

Second, the majority of psalms identified as "imprecatory" are community psalms—expressing the voice of the gathered community of faith—not individual psalms expressing the voice of an individual. Psalms 12, 58, 83, 129, and 137 all express the voice of the community.[17] This reality means that we cannot write the imprecatory passages off as the excesses of ancient individuals, but must come to terms with them as part of the canon.

Third, as we seek ways to answer the question, Why the imprecatory psalms? and, Why and how should we incorporate them into our worship events? we must keep in mind that the cries for vengeance in the psalms are not about lesser or greater conflicts that could be resolved by generosity on the part of the ones praying or through "turning the other cheek." Those who pray these psalms are shouting out their suffering because of the overwhelming injustices and abject indifferences of their foes, their enemies. Zenger writes, "The psalmists confront their God with the mystery of evil and the contradiction represented by evil persons in a world that is in the care of God."[18] The psalm singers cry out to God in the midst of an unjust world—a world in which poverty, oppression, violence, and frightful indifference seem to be ever with them.

Fourth, in the imprecatory psalms, the psalmists call on God to mete out punishment. The imprecatory words of the Psalter are cries to God to "make things right" in the face of seemingly hopeless wrong; they are not cries from communities and individuals for permission to carry out their own retributive acts for the wrongs done to them.

The Imprecatory Psalms and Our Context

Poverty, oppression, violence, exploitation, and frightful indifference—the pages of our newspapers, the cover stories of our Web pages, the headlines on National Public Radio remind us daily of the goings-on in our world. Most of the readers of this essay have never been confronted in a personal way with such foes and enemies. But, perhaps the shrinking world in which we live has given us a new perspective. Perhaps the ever-present starvation, oppression, and exploitation of innocent people throughout the world has given us a new outlook. Perhaps the growing crime rates and poverty in our cities and suburbs has required a new view of things. Perhaps the increasing corruption of our political and corporate leaders, the growing unrest in the world, the downward spiral of morals and ethics, and the declining health of this planet have made us more aware of the declining "rightness" of this world in which we live.

What should be the response of the faithful? Is there a place for imprecation against the enemies of just and right and faithful living? Is there a time for congregations of God's faithful to feel outrage and disbelief and to express words of vengeance? Might we intone the words of Psalm 58?

> Let [the wicked] vanish like water that runs away;
>   like grass let them be trodden down and wither.
> Let them be like the snail that dissolves into slime,
>   like the untimely birth that never sees the sun.
> . . . .
> The righteous will rejoice when they see vengeance done;
>   they will bathe their feet in the blood of the wicked. (vv.
>   7-8, 10)

Or do the faithful, along with the Prioress of Dachau, embrace only words of love and hopefulness in the biblical text? In *Performing the Psalms*, John Mark Hicks writes,

> The reality of a victimized world must be taken seriously, especially when structures of power oppress the poor. Psalm 58 evokes a vision of God's justice that takes the side of the oppressed over against those who abuse their power. It challenges us to enter into their experience and cry to the Lord with them. It challenges us to seek God's kingdom and God's righteousness. . . . It expresses righteous indignation against structural injustice within society.[19]

Walter Brueggemann maintains that the community lament psalms (and, I add, especially the imprecatory psalms) are a complaint that makes the shrill insistence to God that:

1. Things are not right in the present arrangement.
2. They need not stay this way and can be changed.
3. The psalm singer will not accept them in this way, for the present arrangement is intolerable.
4. It is God's obligation to change things.[20]

How *do* we incorporate such cries for justice, such laments over injustices, into the worship of our communities of faith? How do we incorporate such cries into our understanding of the God we worship? For some reason, private lamenting seems acceptable in our faith communities; we feel free in the solitude of our individual prayer lives to say, with the psalmist in Psalm 17:

> Hear a just cause, O Lord; attend to my cry;
> > give ear to my prayer from lips free of deceit.
> From you let my vindication come;
> > let your eyes see the right. (vv. 1-2)

But we are reluctant to voice in community words such as we find in Psalm 94:

> O Lord, you God of vengeance,
> > you God of vengeance, shine forth!
> Rise up, O judge of the earth;
> > give to the proud what they deserve!
> O Lord, how long shall the wicked,
> > how long shall the wicked exult? (vv. 1-3)

Do we feel that our coming together to seek out and understand God in our corporate worship and corporate study of God is too sacred, too otherworldly, too much outside the realm of everyday life, too polite, or too politically correct? We gather, after all, to worship and praise God. But what if praise is not what we feel? What if we have been subjected to atrocities that simply do not allow praise and worship? What then? What did and do the victims of the Holocaust and their descendants feel? What did and do the victims of the race wars in America and their descendants feel? What about parents and children in Darfur and Iraq and other areas of unrest in our world? How do the victims of violent crimes, hate crimes, and fraud feel? And what about children who are victims of sexual and other types of abuse?

The imprecatory psalms remind us of the basic human desire for revenge when we or those we love have been wronged. Such words in the biblical text indicate to us that God does not ask us to suppress those emotions but rather to speak about them in plain and heartfelt terms. In speaking out, we give voice to the pain, the feelings of helplessness, and the burning anger. J. Clinton McCann writes of Psalm 137 in *A Theological Introduction to the Book of Psalms*:

> In the face of monstrous evil, the worst possible response is to feel nothing. What must be felt is grief, rage, and outrage. In their absence, evil becomes an acceptable commonplace. To forget is to submit to evil, to wither and die; to remember is to resist, be faithful, and live again. . . . The psalmist in Psalm 137 submits the anger to God. This submission of anger to God obviates the need for actual revenge on the enemy. For survivors of victimization, to express grief and rage and outrage is to live—to remember is to bear the pain of reliving an unutterable horror—a cross. But to remember is also to resist the forces of evil in the hope of living again—resurrection.[21]

The imprecatory psalms of the Psalter, the imprecatory words of the Psalter, and such words in the Old and New Testaments bespeak an aspect of reality with which all humanity has grappled since the beginning of time. Our ancestors in the faith reflected on the beginning of time in the biblical text. At each stage of the creation story in Genesis 1, God declares creation "good" (vv. 4, 10, 12, 18, 21, 25). And at the completion of that creation story, God declares creation "very good" (v. 31). In the more "earthy" story of creation in Genesis 2, however, God declares that it is "not good" for the human to be alone in the garden (v. 18). God creates a partner for the human as the solution for the "not good" dilemma.

Thus the questions arise. If God created this world as "good" and "very good," then how does humanity explain violence and hatred and unexplained suffering? If God created a good world, then why do atrocities happen; why are children exploited; why do people die from horrendous diseases? The imprecatory psalms and words of imprecation in other passages in the Bible have to do with questions of theodicy—questions of the source of and solution for evil in the world. The answer to the questions? If God created the world good and if God is the sole authority over all that takes place in the world, then the not good in this world can be alleviated by the action of God, just as the original not good was alleviated by the creation of the partner for the first human.

God alone can set the not good right. And thus the psalmists can cry out to God to crush their foes, admonish their enemies, and restore the good of creation. How then do we appropriate the imprecatory psalms into our life of faith, into our theology, into the fabric of our communal being as the people of God? Five thoughts on this matter.

First, Patrick Miller writes, in an essay titled "The Hermeneutics of Imprecation," that a congregation who regularly hears sermons and lessons on psalms will find the imprecatory psalms easier to appropriate into their life of faith. In that way, says Miller, the imprecatory psalms and verses are

> placed in a larger context. . . . They are abrasive pieces of a larger whole and not lifted up to a special place or made a point of focus by reading them by themselves. The rage is clear, but it is set in the context of all the psalms and in the constant listening of the congregation to the images, the deep emotions, the hyperbole—to all the strong and intense language of the Psalms.[22]

Second, congregations must understand the nature of poetry in general and of Hebrew poetry in particular. The Psalter is poetry. And it must be read and interpreted as such. Poetry is evocative, emotional, image-filled, and replete with hyperbole, and it cannot, must not, be read literally. Thus, the words of Psalm 83 must be understood in their poetic context:

O my God, make them like whirling dust,
  like chaff before the wind.
As fire consumes the forest,
    as the flame sets the mountains ablaze,
so pursue them with your tempest
    and terrify them with your hurricane. (vv. 13-15)

A recognition of the imprecatory psalms' poetic qualities are not meant to diminish their raw and heartfelt depths. But their poetic nature must be understood by their hearers.

Third, positing or suggesting historical settings for the imprecatory words will help congregations ground them in a real-life story world. They provide "initial hooks" for hearers—a reminder that the cries for vengeance in the psalms are not about lesser or greater conflicts that could be resolved by generosity on the part of the one praying or through "turning the other cheek." The singers of these psalms are shouting out their suffering because of the overwhelming injustices and abject indifferences of their foes, their enemies.

Fourth, the words of the imprecatory psalms are words of giving over as much as they are words of crying out. As McCann says, monstrous evil *does* take place in our world. It hurts. We must speak out against injustice, inequality, and acts of violence. And in that speaking out, we give the anger and rage over to God. Zenger maintains that Psalm 137, for example, is an attempt, in the face of the most profound humiliation and helplessness, to suppress the primitive human lust for violence in one's own heart by surrendering everything to God—a God whose word of judgment is presumed to be so universally just that even those who pray the psalm submit themselves to it.[23]

Fifth, and most important, giving the anger and the rage over to God does not absolve humanity of responsibility for the source of the anger and rage. When and to what extent do we act ourselves and what do we commit to the safekeeping of the God of all creation? Giving the outrage over to God does not mean giving the responsibility of the community over to God. With giving over comes not, in the words of Clint McCann, acceptance, capitulation, and indifference. With giving over comes moving past the need for human vengeance and moving on to working to make sure that the source of what brought on the imprecatory words never happens again.

As long as people are angry and vengeful against the leaders of those countries who deprive their citizens of the basic human needs of food, water, and shelter, we will never have the energy to find ways to provide folk with those basic needs. As long as we are angry and feel vengeful against those who commit violent crimes, we will never have the energy to move out into our communities and work to eradicate the root causes of those violent crimes. As long as we harbor absolute and abhorrent hate for those who commit terrorist acts, we will never have the energy to attempt to build bridges across the great divide of our worldviews.

The imprecatory psalms are heartfelt, raw, angry, and difficult. Do they need to be heard? Do they need to be studied and preached and taught? Do they yield an insight into the nature and character of the God we worship? The answer to all three questions is yes. For, God knows, we need to cry out; God knows, we need to let go; and God knows, we need to work in our world to end the source of the crying out. And if we do not, then God help us all.

CHAPTER 6

Saying Amen to Violent Psalms: Patterns of Prayer, Belief, and Action in the Psalter

Joel M. LeMon

Introduction: The Psalms as a Source for Theology and Ethics

As a collection of prayers, the book of Psalms has encouraged wide-ranging theological and religio-historical exploration. Ethical analysis, however, has remained a somewhat less-frequent mode of inquiry.[1] Yet the richness of the Psalms' theological claims makes ethical investigations of the book all the more important. For the Psalms' original audiences, as for us today, *how* one prays both affects and reflects *what* one believes.[2] A Latin dictum in the Christian theological tradition relates this principle: *lex orandi lex credendi*, "the pattern (or rule) of prayer is the pattern of belief."[3] Modern liturgical theology—one thinks especially of the work of Geoffrey Wainwright, Don Saliers, and Edward Phillips—has taken the dictum to its necessary conclusion: that the patterns of prayer and belief shape patterns of behavior and action: *lex agendi*.[4]

These patterns of prayer, belief, and action are indeed tightly interwoven. Let us think, for example, about the range of theological and ethical outcomes that results from voicing a psalm of praise.

How does a text like Psalm 146 shape the moral imagination of a community that utters it within the context of prayer?[5]

> Happy are those whose help is the God of Jacob,
>   whose hope is in the LORD their God,
> who made heaven and earth,
>   the sea, and all that is in them,
> who keeps faith for ever;
>   who executes justice for the oppressed,
>   who gives food to the hungry.
>
> The LORD sets the prisoners free;
>   the LORD opens the eyes of the blind.
> The LORD lifts up those who are bowed down;
>   the LORD loves the righteous.
> The LORD watches over the strangers;
>   he upholds the orphan and the widow,
>   but the way of the wicked he brings to ruin. (146:5-9)[6]

According to the theo-logic of the psalm, God deserves praise because of God's work on behalf of those who are powerless, oppressed, or otherwise in need. God's power to do such things derives from God's creative work (v. 6a) and willingness to engage in relationships with humanity (vv. 5, 6b-9).[7]

The theological claims of the psalm have an impact on those who recite it. The act of extolling God (*lex orandi*) as one who helps the weak clearly shapes who the community believes God is (*lex credendi*). Moreover, as the psalm engenders beliefs about God's character and activities, these beliefs can also have an effect on the character and activities of the faithful. If the community continually testifies that God upholds the widow and the fatherless, then those who pray this way are ultimately more likely to act like the God whom they worship. They take care of the needy too. Descriptions about the nature of God, especially in the context of prayer, shape the nature of the person uttering them. If one expects God to act with kindness and care for the lowly, then the ethical implications of such beliefs are clear: one should respond as God would to

the suffering one faces in the world. Put simply, if God gives food
to the hungry (v. 7), then so shall we. In short, the words we utter
about God and especially *to* God shape our behavior.

The authors and editors of the Psalter clearly recognized that
ethics are linked inextricably to the forms and content of prayer.
The implicit connection between ethics and prayer can be seen in
the very structure of the book of Psalms; indeed, the five books of
the Psalter (Pss 1–41, 42–72, 73–89, 90–106, 107–50) reflect the
fivefold division of the Torah (Genesis–Deuteronomy).[8] Within
this framework, numerous psalms describe the benefits of living
according to the law and the overall necessity of righteous behavior. Gordon Wenham has helpfully identified the areas where
individual psalms overlap with aspects of the Decalogue, which
he calls "the quintessence of biblical ethics."[9] With the injunc-
tion to keep Sabbath as the only exception, the book of Psalms
provides numerous affirmations of the precepts of the Decalogue
in poetic form. The net effect of these congruencies between the
Decalogue and the Psalter is that these two nodal points of Old
Testament ethics and piety provide a remarkably consonant picture of what it means to be righteous. Likewise, the portrait of
wickedness emerges in the Psalter as the opposite of righteous
behavior. With the paradigmatic righteous person as one who
unfailingly keeps the law, the wicked one consistently breaks the
Decalogue.

The concern for the law is also obviously the primary focus of
the so-called Torah Psalms (1, 19, and 119).[10] Among the Torah
Psalms, Psalm 1 has pride of place. Indeed, recent scholarship on
the shape and shaping of the Psalter confirms the notion that Psalm
1 sets the agenda for all that follows.[11]

> Happy are those
>> who do not follow the advice of the wicked,
> or take the path that sinners tread,
>> or sit in the seat of scoffers;
> but their delight is in the law of the LORD,
>> and on his law they meditate day and night.

They are like trees
> planted by streams of water,
which yield their fruit in its season,
> and their leaves do not wither.
In all that they do, they prosper.

The wicked are not so,
> but are like chaff that the wind drives away.
Therefore the wicked will not stand in the judgment,
> nor sinners in the congregation of the righteous;
for the LORD watches over the way of the righteous,
> but the way of the wicked will perish. (1:1-6)

The first verses of this psalm reveal a clear ethical decision facing all individuals regarding how they will live within the world. One option is to live with and like the wicked (1:1). However, such a life leads inexorably to destruction (1:4-5, 6b). The other option is to live righteously and enjoy the rich blessings of God as a result (1:2-3; 6a). Given the extreme consequences of these options, it may seem surprising that the psalm names only one specific behavior or activity that characterizes the righteous life; namely, *meditating on the law* (v. 2).

But what does it mean to mediate on the law? Modern readers often understand "meditation" as the process of entering into a state of silence—and especially silence that is tranquil, solitary, and even transcendental. The Hebrew verb *hāgâ* (often translated "meditate," as in NRSV) actually suggests none of these connotations. Rather, *hagah* has a broad semantic range that includes numerous modes of *speaking*: uttering, reciting, growling, murmuring, and even singing.[12] In Ps 1:2, the object of this speech (*hāgâ*) is God's law (*tôrâ*). Thus to *meditate* on the law is to use a wide variety of forms of speech to *talk* about God's justice. While the subject of the meditation is clear (the *tôrâ*), Psalm 1 does not describe who constitutes the audience of the speech. By not describing the audience, the act of meditation becomes a particularly open act of speaking that includes a wide range of audiences: the community, God, the enemy, even the natural world. In fact, that which follows Psalm 1 helps to define what meditation is. Meditation on the law of God means *doing the Psalms*. Put differently, the essence of meditation on the law is prayer: speech to God and about God's justice. Framed this way, the entire Psalter becomes an extended meditation on the law, or the law of God in prayer and song.

In light of Psalm 1, the Psalter presents a thoroughgoing *ethic of prayer*. The careful reader of the Psalms realizes that prayer is the sole foundation of ethical behavior. Prayer informs and shapes every action in the lives of the faithful. And according to the Psalms, right actions rely on constant dialogue with God. So again, one sees confirmation of the principle *lex orandi, lex credendi, lex agendi*. Indeed, the interrelationship of the patterns of prayer, belief, and action constitutes an implicit principle underlying the entire book of Psalms.

Recognizing the ethic of prayer within the Psalms is an important step for doing biblical theology and understanding its impact on Christian praxis. Yet there remains a significant challenge for all those who would pattern their lives after the piety of the Psalms. The challenge comes via the images of violence pervading the Psalter. Violence appears within in a variety of contexts and, indeed, permeates all the genres within the Psalms. Lament psalms, for one, typically describe the wicked devising and inflicting violence on the psalmist. Yet, in these texts, the psalmist often also entreats *God* to perpetrate violence—violence that simultaneously saves the psalmist and deals out retribution against the enemies. These violent pleas—for example, that God would slay the wicked (139:19) or shatter the heads of the enemies (68:21)—create unease among those who would look to the Psalms as a source for ethics today.

In the royal psalms, matters present themselves slightly differently. These texts prove even more difficult as a source for ethical reflection. One finds numerous descriptions of the king executing God's justice on the enemies through imagery shot through with violence. A particularly difficult text is Psalm 18, where divine agency and human agency are conflated in acts of violence against enemies.

I pursued my enemies and overtook them;
    and did not turn back until they were consumed.
I struck them down, so that they were not able to rise;
    they fell under my feet.
For you girded me with strength for the battle;
    you made my assailants sink under me.
You made my enemies turn their backs to me,
    and those who hated me I destroyed.
They cried for help, but there was no one to save them;
    they cried to the LORD, but he did not answer them.
I beat them fine, like dust before the wind;
    I cast them out like the mire of the streets. (18:37-42)

Images of violence even appear in hymns of praise, such as the stirring Psalm 149, which describes a righteous, worshiping community meting out retribution.

Let the high praises of God be in their throats,
    and two-edged swords in their hand,
to execute vengeance on the nations,
    and punishment on the peoples;
to bind their kings with chains,
    and their nobles with fetters of iron;
to execute on them the judgment decreed.
    This is glory for all his faithful ones.
Praise the LORD! (149:6–9)

One wonders, quite simply, are the psalmists right to pray this way and should modern communities of faith, whether Christians or Jews, pray this way too? Furthermore, if one does pray this way, what effect do these prayers have on one's moral imagination? What is the relationship between *lex orandi* and *lex agendi* when it comes to violent prayer?

The Appropriation of Violent Psalms

There have, of course, been many suggestions for how one should understand the violent imagery in the Psalms and what role, if any, these troubling texts should play in the piety of today's Christian communities.[13]

One exceedingly common tactic for dealing with these "problematic" psalms is simply to exclude them from the liturgy of worshiping communities, which still happens in many Christian traditions. A quick glance through mainline songbooks such as the United Methodist hymnal and the Presbyterian (PC[USA]) hymnal reveals that most depictions of divine violence are not included in the responsorial readings and the Psalms settings.[14] Similarly, the psalms lections in the Revised Common Lectionary exclude most of the pleas for God to exact violence on enemies.[15] This practice of excluding violent imagery arose not simply from the wary hymnal editors, pastors, and church musicians. Psalms scholarship—at least until the mid-twentieth century—informed the practice, at least in part. For example, W. O. E. Oesterley argues for the inappropriateness and the "outrage on religion" in the last verses of Psalm 137. He reckons the author to be "a man of passionate feelings, and among the best of those with a temperament like that, evil will at times predominate."[16] For Oesterley, it is simply *evil* to bash babies against rocks—even Babylonian babies. And surely it follows that no evil prayers should be a part of Christian piety.

Many other scholars have judged the violent strains of Ps 137:9 to be evil, along with a host of similar violent prayers throughout the Psalter. Artur Weiser, for example, has this to say about the image of the righteous celebrating God's vindication and bathing their feet in the blood of the wicked in Ps 58:10-11: "The psalm's conclusion . . . shows . . . the undisguised gloating and cruel vindictiveness of an intolerant religious fanaticism; it is one of those dangerous poisonous blossoms which are liable to grow even on the tree of religious knowledge and clearly show the limits set to the Old Testament religion."[17]

Within this and many other interpretations, one can perceive a clear supercessionist tone; that is, a sense that the Christian community has now replaced the Jews as God's chosen people and that the covenant with Abraham has been eradicated by the new covenant in Jesus Christ. Thus, for example, these so-called psalms of imprecation—the cursing psalms—seem to stem from a pre-Christian or even anti-Christian Judaism, a religion at best out of tune with Christianity and at best utterly contrary to Jesus's teaching of love for one's enemies (see Matt 5:4; Luke 6:27, 35).[18] Erich Zenger is correct to identify these perspectives as the legacy of Marcion.[19] In some of its many forms, supersessionism condemns Jewish religion because of the Old Testament's ostensibly violent and vindictive image of God, one which was "abolished and destroyed" by the revelation of God in Jesus.[20] In this ideology, the image of a bloodthirsty, vindictive God of Israel is easily projected on to the "bloodthirsty Jews" and vice versa. It is truly a sad irony that this skewed vision of "the Old Testament God" and "the Jews" has informed, justified, and even motivated horrific, brutal acts of violence against Jews at the hands of Christians.[21]

Clearly, the ethical implications of simply rejecting violent psalms and/or violent portions of psalms make this tactic an unacceptable option. Thus, a common trend among biblical scholars is to identify ways of voicing and reckoning with the violent imagery of the Psalms. One can understand this move as a part of a larger effort to reclaim the full scope of the Psalter as appropriate and even vital to Christian piety.[22] One approach to these psalms draws from the field of psychology, understanding the violent pleas of the psalmist as a form of catharsis. According to this line of thinking, violent thoughts that go unacknowledged degrade and pollute the relationship between God and the supplicant. Faithfulness requires praying honestly and voicing all of one's feelings before God, even those about retribution. Thus, these psalms function as a form of theological catharsis for those who suffer greatly.[23] Similarly, Patrick Miller has suggested that psalms of imprecation are valuable for Christian faith and practice in that they represent a simultaneous "letting go" and "holding back." The prayers validate the experience of suffering and acknowledge the need for retribution, even as the psalmists restrain their emotions by *praying* the violence rather than executing violence themselves.[24]

Yet another approach is to reframe the language and imagery of violence in the Psalter such that these violent psalms ultimately reflect the supplicant's commitment to God's justice. Erich Zenger's work best reflects this notion. For him, semantics are critical in framing the argument. He suggests that one must not conflate the modern notions of vengeance with punishment and justice. Rather than portraying a picture of Israel's God as a vindictive deity, the psalmists picture God as profoundly and unflinchingly just, a status that necessitates some form of punishment for those who upset the right order that God has established. Thus, pleas for God to act violently are essentially faithful statements about the ultimate outcomes of God's righteousness. Zenger argues that the " 'psalms of enmity' are a way of robbing the aggressive images of the enemies of their destructiveness, and transforming them into constructive forces."[25] Furthermore, Zenger claims, the psalms as prayers should not be understood as the Word of God in any way that would condone such acts of violence, but the psalms rather provide testimony about God's just nature. They inform who God is, but in an oblique way, in poetry and in prayer, not in systematic theological terms.

Still other interpreters, like David Firth for example, suggest that the violent imagery, like the large body of legal material in the Old Testament, places an accent on the *measured* response to the violence of the wicked. The violent psalms essentially reflect *lex talionis*.[26] This principle of "an eye for an eye" actually signals a restraint on victims of violence whose natural inclinations might be to take "a head for an eye." Moreover, Firth has argued that the execution of *lex talionis* is left entirely to God—at least in the individual lament psalms. Thus, these psalms, in fact, present a radical ethic of nonviolence. By placing violence in the context of prayer, the psalmists reject the right of human retribution and trust in God alone to bring about justice.[27] The psalmists leave the judgment up to God, putting down the swords, nets, and clubs and lifting up their voices in prayer.

Both Ellen Davis and Erhard Gerstenberger identify other positive ethical outcomes of reading and praying the psalms of imprecation; namely, that such psalms have the effect of helping communities identify *themselves* as perpetuators of violence. Davis suggests that the striking images of violence in the imprecatory psalms raise the important question of whether or not there are those who would pray this way against us.[28] Gerstenberger, writing from a liberationist perspective, argues that the benefit of the psalms is their seeking to identify the enemy. He argues that those in the northern hemisphere do not typically identify the enemy when they see the world's suffering. "Instead they identify charity as the way to address the suffering. If they were to identify the enemy, they would realize that they are the enemy."[29] Roland E. Murphy voices a similar sentiment. When violent wishes are "heard in prayer, they illumine our own feelings, and even . . . accuse us of our own acts of vengeance."[30] In sum, according to each of these three interpreters, the psalms in one way or another hold a mirror to their readers and prompt introspection about the causes of violence and the nature of enmity.

Assessing the Tactics

Each of these responses to the problem of violence in the Psalms has its merits, yet questions still remain. First, one must admit that the principle of *lex talionis* seems not to operate in every case, even in the individual psalms of lament. In some psalms, the violence against the enemies for which the psalmists pray seems woefully out of balance with the threat that the enemies seem to pose. For example, Psalm 17, a prayer of one falsely accused, describes the judgment of God as a bottled up reservoir of wrath, that once released destroys the accusers, their children, and their grandchildren.

> Rise up, Yahweh, confront his face. Bow him down.
>> Deliver my life from the wicked by your sword.
> From humans—by your hand—O Yahweh,
>> From humans, whose portion in life comes from the world.
> And with your reserves you will fill their belly.

Their sons will be sated,
And they will leave their remainder for their children.
        (17:13-14)[31]

Moving beyond the genre of individual laments, as Firth constrains it,[32] the principle of *lex talionis* seems not to be so thoroughly worked in the rest of the Psalter. *Lex talionis* does seem to be operative in Ps 137:8, "blessed is the one who pays you back for what you have done to us." Yet *lex talionis* is difficult to perceive in other graphic images of the enemies' demise, such as that portrayed in Psalm 58. It is exceedingly difficult to maintain that the Psalms reject any act of retribution by humans against humans when the full scope of the Psalter is taken into account. While Yahweh most commonly appears as the one who will execute violence on the enemies (e.g., Psalm 46), in several psalms humans mete out violence, often the king (as in Psalms 2, 18; 45:5) but also the community, as in Psalm 149, cited earlier. Zenger is right to call into question the semantics of conflating retribution, justice, and vengeance. Yet even so, these psalms suggest that violence at the hands of humans can serve the will of a righteous, judging God. Sadly, we have seen this ideology employed over and over again both in antiquity and in our own times, both on the lips of our enemies and our own leaders.

As noted earlier, a community's patterns of prayer both reflect and inform its behavior: *lex orandi, lex credendi, lex agendi*. When one praises Yahweh as the helper of widows, orphans, prisoners, and the downtrodden (146:8-9), over time those prayers shape the supplicant. Thus, one who prays that way will more likely minister to the needs of these people just as God does. This positive ethical outcome of prayer can, however, have a negative reflex as well. When one prays for God to execute violence on evil oppressors, the moral imagination of the supplicant is liable to embrace only the picture of God's dealing deadly blows to the enemies. This person may be motivated to act as God's agent of vengeance if and when the supplicant has the power to do so. In this way, violent prayers can have an ultimately deleterious effect.[33]

A powerful illustration of these potentially negative outcomes emerged recently following the murder of a doctor who had been performing abortions in Wichita. In the wake of the murder, a pastor and former officer of a major American denomination announced that he celebrated the death of the doctor. The pastor went on to say that the doctor's death was an answer to prayer: "I said to the Lord, 'Lord, I pray back to you the psalms. . . .' And we began calling for those imprecatory prayers, because he [the "abortion doctor"] had obviously turned his back on God again and again and again."[34] This same pastor gained national media attention for advocating the use "imprecatory prayers" against the leaders of Americans United for Separation of Church and State and even against the President of the United States.[35]

In a recent interview, the pastor said: "This whole concept that we're always to pray little, nice, soft, fluffy, prayers—that we're not to pray imprecatory prayer—has been something that just, in all honesty, that [we] have lost, and we need to regain imprecatory prayer."[36] It would be easy to dismiss this statement as the ravings of an extremist—were it not for the fact that his call for reclaiming imprecation sounds uncomfortably familiar to comments many seminary professors (like myself) regularly utter in the classroom. Hearing this pastor's call for prayers of imprecation, theological educators and Psalms scholars cannot help but ponder the implications of the recent trend of reclaiming the psalms of imprecation in the piety of the church. One is right to worry that, the more people pray the psalms of imprecation, the more likely it is that God will mete out the type of violence against the "enemies" that the imprecatory psalms describe.

Granting and Withholding *Amen*s: The Role of the Community

At this point, the antiphonal nature of the Psalms becomes important for understanding and living out the ethic of prayer that the Psalms suggest. Prayers uttered in a faithful community prompt the community's "Amen." In ancient Israel and in the modern church, Prayer is no individualistic act but relies on a community to say "so be it." In doing so, communities can and should serve as moderators and regulators of prayers.

The Hebrew Bible records several examples of individuals and groups voicing their amens (Num 5:22; Deut 27:15-26; 1 Kgs 1:36; 1 Chron 16:36; Neh 5:13; 8:6; Pss 41:13; 72:19; 89:52; 106:48; Jer 28:6). And within the Psalter, amens come within the benedictory formulas at the end of each of the first four books of the Psalter.

> Blessed be the LORD, the God of Israel,
>> from everlasting to everlasting. Amen and Amen. (41:13)

> Blessed be his glorious name forever;
>> may his glory fill the whole earth. Amen and Amen. (72:19)

> Blessed be the LORD for ever. Amen and Amen. (89:52)

> Blessed be the LORD, the God of Israel,
>> from everlasting to everlasting.
> And let all the people say, "Amen."
>> Praise the LORD! (106:48)

These benedictions textualize the real, living voice of the community. They remind the reader of the lived context of these prayers: these prayers are uttered by real, suffering persons in communities that confirm those prayers with amens. In the Psalms, this mode of interaction between supplicant and community is now only evident at the end of large sections of psalms.

As a way of reckoning with violence inherent in so many psalms, I suggest that, as a practical-theological and ecclesiological matter, the violent psalms *require* a community to adjudicate carefully the propriety of such prayers on the lips of each supplicant. This tactic not only makes good sense from a pastoral perspective. In fact, the Hebrew Bible itself suggests this way of a community appropriating imprecations. One very helpful analogue comes in Deut 27:11-26, in which the Levites declare a series of curses against those who break God's law. Each curse is followed invariably by the community's "Amen."

> The same day Moses charged the people as follows: When you have crossed over the Jordan, these shall stand on Mount Gerizim for the blessing of the people: Simeon, Levi, Judah, Issachar, Joseph, and Benjamin. And these shall stand on Mount Ebal for the curse: Reuben, Gad, Asher, Zebulun, Dan, and Naphtali. Then the Levites shall declare in a loud voice to all the Israelites:
>
> "Cursed be anyone who makes an idol or casts an image, anything abhorrent to the LORD, the work of an artisan, and sets it up in secret." All the people shall respond, saying, "Amen!"
>
> "Cursed be anyone who dishonors father or mother." All the people shall say, "Amen!"
>
> "Cursed be anyone who moves a neighbor's boundary marker." All the people shall say, "Amen!"
>
> "Cursed be anyone who misleads a blind person on the road." All the people shall say, "Amen!"
>
> "Cursed be anyone who deprives the alien, the orphan, and the widow of justice." All the people shall say, "Amen!"
>
> "Cursed be anyone who lies with his father's wife, because he has violated his father's rights." All the people shall say, "Amen!"
>
> "Cursed be anyone who lies with any animal." All the people shall say, "Amen!"
>
> "Cursed be anyone who lies with his sister, whether the daughter of his father or the daughter of his mother." All the people shall say, "Amen!"
>
> "Cursed be anyone who lies with his mother-in-law." All the people shall say, "Amen!"
>
> "Cursed be anyone who strikes down a neighbor in secret." All the people shall say, "Amen!"
>
> "Cursed be anyone who takes a bribe to shed innocent blood." All the people shall say, "Amen!"
>
> "Cursed be anyone who does not uphold the words of this law by observing them." All the people shall say, "Amen!" (Deut 27:11-26)

For our purposes here, the content of the curses is not as important as their general tone and the community's response to them. The imprecations against those who break God's law receive confirmation from the community. Curses have a uniquely powerful rhetorical force within the community, and thus the curses need the force of the community behind them to confirm their efficaciousness. It is particularly noteworthy that the community does not reply with the same amen formula to the litany of blessings in Deuteronomy 28, which follow the curses. Curses, it seems, are particularly susceptible to misappropriation, so that the community must play a critical role of confirming them.[37]

As with the litany of curses in Deuteronomy 27, the psalms of imprecation (and the psalms describing violence against the enemies more generally) demand a community's response—a community that regulates these psalms with its amens. The amens in the Psalter *do not* come at the end of each individual prayer. Instead, they only appear at the conclusions of the first four books. At these conclusions, the community's voice in support of the prayers is heard. It is not every individual prayer that receives the community's amen, but the whole scope of prayers in an entire book of psalms. In other words, it is the books of Psalms *in aggregate* that the editors confirm with the community's amens. In order for there to be a communal amen for each particular psalm, there must be an actual, real, that is to say, nontextualized community ready for response.

If the Psalms themselves leave the responsibility of confirming prayers to the living, reading community, how then should modern communities discern the appropriateness of any given prayer? How should the community know when to say amen? The community must realize that prayer requires honesty before God, and sometimes one honestly desires the destruction of one's enemies because of the acuteness of the pain and depth of the fear one experiences as a result of oppression. When the community identifies that the pain, fear, or anxiety of the supplicant is indeed merited and that the expression of the violent desires are a necessary—even cathartic—step in healing, then the community may respond to a violent prayer with its amen. However, a community might also sense a tension between the level of vindictiveness expressed in the prayer and the real experience of the one praying that way. That is to say, the community may recognize that the supplicant's desire for retribution is out of balance with the level of suffering. In such cases, the community would rightly withhold its amen from one supplicant. It is possible, however, that the same imprecatory prayer might come from the mouth of another sufferer whose desperate situation would indeed prompt the confirmation of the community with an amen.

A community should realize that violent psalms reflect the emotions of those at their weakest state, who, given the threat of their enemies, are in no position to fight back through their own power. The psalms of imprecation are the prayers of the powerless, whose only source of strength is the hope that God will act powerfully for their salvation. In such a desperate position, it is difficult to imagine that salvation from enemies would come in any other form than violence against them. The conflation of pleas of salvation from and violence against enemies is completely understandable in these cases. When the powerless utter these prayers, the community is right to grant an amen. However, if a powerful person prays this way, the risks are greater that that individual might muster his or her energies and attempt to serve the will of God by executing violence on his enemies. Such a prayer from a comparatively powerful supplicant would receive only a tentative amen or none at all.

The sensitive, faithful, and inspired community always affirms that praying is good. As Psalm 1 suggests, prayer is *the* essential element required for the righteous, moral life. Part of the goodness of prayer is that it opens up a dialogue, not just between God and the supplicant, but between the supplicant and the community. With its amens, the community is able to confirm that it is always better to pray for God to act violently against enemies than it is for the supplicant to take matters into her or his own hands. The sensitive community is aware both that violent prayers have value and also that they can be abused, for example, when nonvictims pray for

God's violent judgment, or when a victim might be tempted not to trust God to do the work of justice.

Recent Psalms scholarship suggests that modern Christian communities should reclaim the full scope of the Psalter as a source for piety. If this is to happen, a robust ecclesiology is essential, one that emphasizes the critical responsibility of communities to take their amens seriously. Communities confirm, regulate, and moderate the prayers that emerge from within them. When one prays the imprecatory psalms, the burden lies on the community to be sensitive to the range of ethical implications of these prayers. The community's process of evaluating prayers comes through its understanding of the full revelation of God in Jesus Christ, the entire witness of Scripture, and sensitivity to power of the Holy Spirit to guide its deliberations and judgments. This inspired community should understand the full range of ways that prayer can shape the moral imagination and realize the inextricable link between ethics and prayer.

CHAPTER 7

"The Faithfulness of the Lord Endures Forever": The Theological Witness of the Psalter

Rolf A. Jacobson

For both Christians and Jews, the Psalms have played and continue to play a central role in life of faith. The Psalter provides intimate prayers that believers pray to interact with God—in times of crisis, doubt, and joy. The Psalter also provides liturgies and hymns that shape the practices and beliefs of people who come together in God's presence for worship. The Psalter offers promises about who God is, who humanity is in light of God, and who we should (and should not be) for each other. All of this leads to a rather basic question: What vision of God emerges when one submerges oneself in the prayers, songs, liturgies, and poems in the Psalter?[1] What God does one meet in the many and various poems of this collection? What does the Psalter as a whole confess about God? This essay explores these questions.

I believe that the dominant theological confession of the Psalter may be summed up concisely as *The Lord is faithful*. In this essay,

I explore this basic confession of the Lord's faithfulness as one of faith in a living God—that is, through the prayers, songs, liturgies, and poems of the Psalter, one encounters the living God, word to word. As human beings pray, sing, read, and recite the Psalter's words, those words *communicate* God. Thus, the question of what sort of God the Psalter confesses is not merely an abstract academic issue but a rather concrete issue for faith and theology.

The Semantic Field of "Faithfulness/Fidelity"

The shortest of all the psalms, Psalm 117, provides a convenient place to begin unpacking the Psalter's assertion that Israel has been elected and become enmeshed with a faithful God. This staccato call to praise, with no time to spare for verbosity, abbreviates its theological witness and in the process points us to the basis of all of Israel's praise:

> Praise the LORD, all you nations!
>   Extol him, all you peoples!
> For great is his steadfast love toward us,
>   and the faithfulness of the LORD endures forever.
> Praise the LORD!

The heart of Psalm 117 is also the core of the Psalter's confession about God; namely, that the Lord is a God of steadfast love—*ḥesed*—and enduring faithfulness—*ʾĕmet*. The terms often appear in parallel with each other (for example, Pss 25:10; 26:3; 40:10-11; 57:10). When it comes to interpreting the Bible, my heart is normally left strangely unwarmed by arguments based on statistical data. But in this case, it seems at worth noting that of the roughly 255 occurrences of the term *ḥesed* in the Masoretic Text, 130 of those occur in the Psalter. Over half of all the occurrences of one of Israel's most deeply theological terms occur in the Psalms! This statistical datum, then, offers at least some support for the claim that the faithfulness of the Lord is the Psalter's dominant witness. The pair of words (*ḥesed* and *ʾĕmet*) also often appear in parallel with a further core set of theologically weighted terms: *ṣedeq/ṣĕdāqâ*, "righteous/righteous-ness" (see 85:10-11); *yĕšûʿâ*, "salvation/deliverance" (see 69:14); *reḥem*, "mercy" (see 86:15); *ḥānan*, "grace" (cf. 86:15); *mišpāṭ*, "just/justice" (see 111:7); *ṭôb/ṭôbâ*, "good/goodness" (see 136:1); and *ʾĕmûnâ*, "faithfulness/trustworthiness" (see 100:5; 89:49). Altogether, this family of terms charts out a semantic field that begins to outline the Psalter's vision of God. The English word that best describes the semantic field that all of these Hebrew terms together chart out is *fidelity*. And the English sentence that best sums up the Psalter's use of these terms is "the Lord is faithful." The semantic field in question bears witness to the Psalter's confession that when the creator Lord enters into relationship with individuals, with the chosen people as a whole, and with creation, these divine-creaturely relationships have a discernable and predictable character. This is so because God is one of the partners in these relationships, and God has made the divine character known.

The two chief terms under consideration are *ḥesed* and *ʾĕmet*. The first of the two is notoriously difficult to translate. Attempts to capture it in English include "mercy," "fidelity/faithfulness," "loyalty," "love," and so on. Rather than get bogged down in an argument about translation, a more helpful approach is to recognize that *ḥesed* is a *relational term*. It does not merely assert some abstract quality concerning God's inner nature but rather confesses the way that the Lord relates to others. It asserts that the internal character of God is consistent with the way God is in relationship. As the venerable Gerhard von Rad has already noted concerning the term *ḥesed*, it "designates an attitude required by fellowship and includes a disposition and an attitude of solidarity. . . . So it expresses . . . beneficent personal disposition plus the actions that follow."[2] That is, it is a relational term. Philip Melanchthon famously asserted that "to know Christ is to know his benefits, and not . . . to reflect upon his natures."[3] Similar to this, as one charts the Psalter's use of *ḥesed*, the emphasis is on the relational ramification's of God's character. For example, Ps 5:7 confesses that "I, through the abundance of your steadfast love, / will enter your house." Or Ps 21:7 describes of the king that "through the steadfast love of the Most High he shall not be moved." To reiterate the point from Melanchthon, the Psalms confess the benefits of being in relationship with the Lord rather than the Lord's internal natures. The second term, *ʾĕmet*, has at its root the sense of truth. But not truth in the sense of some abstract dictionary definition but truth in the sense of one person in a relationship being truthful to another, or being trustworthy, constant—indeed of being faithful.[4] This relational sense of God's *ʾĕmet* is evident in the expression of trust found in Psalm 31:5, "Into your hand I commit my spirit; / you have redeemed me, O LORD, faithful God [*ʾēl ʾĕmet*]." Or in the plea for deliverance in Psalm 69:13-14: "O God, / in the abundance of your steadfast love [*ḥesed*], answer me. / With your faithful help [*ʾĕmet*], rescue me." The very nature of the Psalms is, in fact, relational. The poems of the Psalter are neither abstract lyrics nor disembodied meditations. They are interpersonal communications with God; they are songs of a community of individuals related both to God and to each other, and they are intrapersonal instruction exploring the delicate web of human, divine, and natural relationships.

The Confession of Faithfulness and the Genres of the Psalter

The confession that God is faithful also provides a helpful point of contact with the concept of the genres of the Psalter. The Psalter's relational view of God and the relational nature of the Psalms themselves provides the intersections at which the various psalm genres meet. Prayers for help (often called laments) in the Psalter are located at the intersection of the confession that God is faithful and some experience of the psalmist that either calls into question God's fidelity or demands a faithful action from God. In that vein, notice the following questions and pleas from the prayers of help:

- Has his steadfast love [*ḥesed*] ceased forever?
  Are his promises at an end for all time? (77:8)

- Turn, O LORD, save my life;
  deliver me for the sake of your steadfast love [*ḥesed*]. (6:4)

- Lord, where is your steadfast love [*ḥesed*] of old,
  which by your faithfulness [*ʾĕmûnâ*] you swore to David?
    (89:49)

- Wondrously show your steadfast love [*ḥesed*],
  O Savior of those who seek refuge
  from their adversaries at your right hand. (17:7)

Similarly, the penitential psalms base pleas for forgiveness on the Lord's faithfulness. They are poems built around the psalmist's recognition that he or she has not acted with faithfulness toward God or neighbor and thus base their pleas solely on the character of the Lord:

- Do not remember the sins of my youth or my transgressions;
  according to your steadfast love [*ḥesed*] remember me,
  for your goodness' [*ṭôb*] sake, O LORD. (25:7)

- Have mercy upon me, O God,
  according to your steadfast love [*ḥesed*];
  according to your abundant mercy [*reḥem*]
  blot out my transgressions. (51:1)

The psalms of trust and the declarations of confidence that occur in prayers for help likewise express confidence in God's fidelity, in spite of looming threats:

- Surely goodness [*ṭôb*] and mercy [*ḥesed*] shall follow me
  all the days of my life. (23:6)

- But I trusted [or "do trust"] in your steadfast love [*ḥesed*];
  my heart shall rejoice in your salvation [*yĕšûʿâ*]. (13:5)

The songs of thanksgiving, on the other hand, are located at the other end of the block, as it were—where a psalmist's experience of deliverance now leads him or her to sing a song confessing the Lord's faithfulness:

- I have told the glad news of deliverance [*ṣedeq*]
     in the great congregation;
  see, I have not restrained my lips,
     as you know, O LORD.
  I have not hidden your saving help [*ṣĕdāqâ*] within my heart,
     I have spoken of your faithfulness [*ʾĕmûnâ*] and your sal-
        vation [*yĕšûʿâ*];
  I have not concealed your steadfast love [*ḥesed*] and your
     faithfulness [*ʾĕmet*]
     from the great congregation. (40:9-10)

- Many are the torments of the wicked,
     but steadfast love [*ḥesed*] surrounds those who trust in the
        LORD. (32:10)

- He will send [or "does send"] from heaven and save me,
     he will put to shame those who hotly pursue me;
  God will send forth his steadfast love [*ḥesed*] and his faithful-
     ness [*ʾĕmet*]. (57:3)

- O give thanks to the LORD, for he is good;
     his steadfast love endures for ever.
  Let the redeemed of the LORD say so,
     those he redeemed from trouble
  and gathered in from the lands,
     from the east and from the west,
     from the north and from the south. (107:1-3)

Similarly, the wisdom psalms (or "instructional psalms") meditate on a long history (both personal and communal) of God's fidelity, and they teach the next generations to trust in God's faithfulness. Thus, the wisdom psalms rest at the intersection between communal experience of and testimony regarding the Lord's fidelity:

- Once God has spoken,
     twice have I heard this:

that power belongs to God,
    and steadfast love [*ḥesed*] to you, O Lord. (62:11-12)

- The earth, O Lord, is filled with your steadfast love [*ḥesed*];
    teach me your statutes. (119:64; cf. vv. 41, 76, 88, 124, 149,
        159).

As already noted, the psalms of praise bear witness to Israel's fundamental conviction that the character of the Lord is the most trustworthy and most defining reality in the universe. These praise songs
live at the intersection of Israel's long experience of God's faithfulness and the community's gatherings in public worship. In addition
to the hymns of praise, the psalms that fit here include the great
festival psalms (50, 81, 95), certain of the liturgies (such as 15, 24,
115, 118, and 121), some of the royal psalms (e.g., 2, 72, 110), and
the historical psalms (78, 105, 106). Again, as already noted, these
psalms' basic theological confession is that the Lord is trustworthy
and faithful:

- I will sing of your loyalty [*ḥesed*] and of justice [*mišpāṭ*];
    to you [or "of you"], O Lord, I will sing. (101:1)

- Steadfast love [*ḥesed*] and faithfulness [*ʾĕmet*] will meet;
    righteousness [*ṣedeq*] and peace will kiss each other.
  Faithfulness [*ʾĕmet*] will spring up from the ground,
    and righteousness [*ṣedeq*] will look down from the sky.
  The Lord will give what is good [*ṭôb*]. (85:10-12)

- For the Lord is good [*ṭôb*];
    his steadfast love [*ḥesed*] endures forever,
    and his faithfulness [*ʾĕmûnâ*] to all generations. (100:5)

These examples could be multiplied many times over. I have offered
this sampling of examples in order to support the assertion that
the vision of the Lord one encounters in the Psalms is a vision of a
God of fidelity. I have also offered this sampling in order to demonstrate, albeit briefly, the manner in which the Psalter's particular view of God has been woven into the fabric of the very genres

of the Psalms. Thus, not only in terms of content but in terms of form, the Psalms bear witness to Israel's basic confession of faith: the Lord is faithful.

Realms of the Lord's Faithfulness

But where is the Lord's fidelity experienced? In what realms is it made available? Psalm 136 provides one likely place to begin the task of exploring these questions. The poem is an antiphonal response psalm in which every other phrase confesses, "For his steadfast love endures forever"—the same characteristic confession of the Lord's fidelity voiced in Psalm 117 and other psalms (cf. Pss 106:1; 107:1; 118:2-4). The first phrase in each of the verses from 136:5-25, then, begin to sketch in the outlines of what God's acts of *ḥesed* are. Broadly speaking, the picture that emerges is of a God whose faithfulness has been experienced in creation (vv. 5-9, 25) and in a history of dealing graciously with the chosen people Israel (vv. 10-24).[5] Psalm 136's characteristic witness to the Lord's fidelity as experienced in both creation and in Israel's history can be further traced both through those psalms known as the creation psalms and the historical psalms, respectively, as well as through many other psalms, such as 46, which pairs the themes of creation and history.

God's Faithfulness Experienced in Creation

As Psalm 33 testifies, the Psalter understands creation as a manifestation of God's faithfulness: "He loves righteousness [*ṣĕdāqâ*] and justice [*mišpāṭ*]; the earth is full of the steadfast love [*ḥesed*] of the LORD" (v. 5). Psalm 33 is one in a set of psalms often identified as "creation psalms" (Psalms 8, 19, 29, 104, 139, and occasionally 148 are also included in this group[6]). The theme of creation is also found in many other psalms (e.g., 139, 89, 68, 102). Although an in-depth study of the theological witness of creation in the Psalms is beyond the scope of this essay, a few insights about the Psalter's understanding of God's faithfulness in the creation material of the Psalms will have to suffice here.[7]

First, the creation psalms testify to God's faithfulness not merely in the existence of creation, *but in the discernible ordering of creation*. Although it would be too much to say that the psalms bear witness to the concept of natural law, the Psalms do bear witness that the Creator has fashioned creation according to certain laws and patterns. One might even say according to logical patterns—"who *by understanding* made the heavens" (136:5), "*in wisdom* you have made them all" (104:24)[8]. This ordering is apparent in such things as the natural cycle of fertility: you "give them their food in due season . . . you open your hand, they are filled with good things" (104:27-28; cf. 145:15-16). The very fact—which we humans almost always take for granted—that we live in the midst of a creation in which the order of things can be trusted is a sign of God's fidelity. The times of sunrise, sunset, and the tides can be known and calculated in advance. The seasons for planting and harvesting, for mating and giving birth, for resting and being active, for growing up, growing mature, and growing old can be planned for—as even the ancient Hebrew inscription known as the Gezer calendar bears witness. God has fashioned a trustworthy creation. In fact, the trustworthiness of creation is a reflection of the character of the Divine One who made it. It is evidence that "the earth is full of the steadfast love [*ḥesed*] of the Lord."

Similarly, God's fidelity within creation is likewise seen in the natural order, in which some creatures are given responsibility and power over others and in the discernible hierarchies that exist between God's many creatures: "You have put all things under their feet, all sheep and oxen, and also the beasts of the field, the birds of the air, and the fish of the sea" (8:6-8).[9] When the creatively endowed hierarchies that are fashioned into creation operate smoothly—so that parents care for children, adults care for the aged, the government takes responsibility for citizens, religious leaders assume stewardship for their flocks, and human beings exercise servant dominion among creation—in all of these domains creation mirrors the faithful character of God.

We can also see God's faithfulness in the complementary roles God assigns various aspects of creation to play: "You set a boundary that [the waters] may not pass, / so that they might not again cover the earth" (104:9). According to Psalm 147, "He sends out his command to the earth, / his word runs swiftly" (v. 15). All of this ordering is a sign of God's faithfulness, because the ordering is necessary for life. Without such ordering, there could be no life. And thus the built-in laws of creation demonstrate faithfulness in God. An additional word should be said here about the theme of God's limiting and ruling over the powers of chaos—"the waters," "the deep," "the flood," "the waves," "the sea," and so on. This is a pervasive theme throughout the Psalter. God limits the powers of chaos but *does not eliminate them.* The language of the Psalms suggests that God rules[10] over these powers *but does not rule them out of creation.* God sets limits beyond which the powers of chaos may not pass, but note that this also implies limits within which the powers of chaos, anticreation, and randomness operate freely. So the ordering laws that God builds into creation are balanced by a randomness and chaos also necessary for creation to thrive.

The Psalms testify that creation provides both a place for life and the means for life to thrive—and that these provisions bear witness to God's fidelity. Psalm 65:9-13 contains an exquisite poetic witness to the way in which God provides for life *through creation.* "You visit the earth and water it . . . you provide the people with grain, for so you have prepared it" (v. 9). Note that God's provision of food is at least one step removed from those whom God feeds. God provides the rain, which allows the earth to provide food, according to God's established order.

> You crown the year with your bounty [*ṭôbâ*]
> . . . .
>   the hills gird themselves with joy
> the meadows clothe themselves with flocks,
>   the valleys deck themselves with grain,
>   they shout and sing together for joy. (vv. 11-13)[11]

God's Faithfulness Experienced in History

Psalm 106, one of the Psalter's historical psalms, begins with the characteristic confession of the Lord's faithfulness, "O give thanks to the LORD, for he is good; / for his steadfast love endures forever." The rest of the psalm connects the history of God's gracious deeds with the conclusion that God's character is faithful. Psalms 106, 78, and 105 are often described as Israel's great historical psalms. But as noted above in regard to the creation psalms, it should be stressed that historical themes are to be found in many other psalms, such as the communal laments (44, 60, 74, 79, 80, 83, 89) and such psalms as 107, 126, 132, and many royal psalms.

Here, I will limit my comments to a threefold outline embedded in the material, and then to some theological implications that emerge from considering the pattern.

The threefold outline is that the history of God's dealings with the people tells a story in which (1) God has repeatedly authored "wonderful works" (78:4, 11-12, 32; 105:2, 5; 106:7, 22; 107:8, 15, 21, 24, 31; niplĕ'ôt); (2) the people have repeatedly proved faithless and rebellious; and (3) God has met each new act of infidelity with unsurpassed fidelity.

The "wonderful works" of the Lord is a shorthand phrase describing the history of God's gracious deeds. Two events are paradigmatic. On the one hand, the saga of the rescue from Egypt, the guidance through wilderness, and the gift of the land (78:12-55; 105:26-42; 106:6-23). And on the other hand, the covenantal promise to David (132:1-18; 89:19-37; 78:68-72). Other events are named or hinted at, including the events of Joseph's life (105:16-25) and the return from exile (126). The point of the historical recitals, of course, is not what happened but that *what happened was God's doing* and that *what God did once has ongoing import.* And underlying all of these "wonderful works" is the concept of divine election. God "chose the tribe of Judah" (78:68) and "has chosen Zion" (132:13); the people are "his chosen ones" (105:43); Moses is "his chosen one" (106:23), and so on. And woven in, with, and under the concept of God's election of Israel is the concept of God's fidelity—that having elected Israel, God is now committed to the relationship and will therefore prove faithful.

Using a stock set of metaphors, the authors of the historical material in the Psalms describe the constant infidelity of the people. Israel "did not keep God's covenant" (78:10); "did not remember the abundance of your steadfast love" (106:7); "forgot what he had done" (78:11; cf. 106:13); "did not wait for his counsel" (106:13); "had no faith in God, / and did not trust his saving power" (78:22; cf. 106:24); "still sinned [and] did not believe in his wonders" (78:32), "did not obey the voice of the LORD" (106:25); "lied to him with their tongues" (78:36); "put God to the test" (106:14); "tested God again and again" (78:41); "sacrificed their sons / and their daughters to the demons" (106:37); "their heart was not steadfast towards him" (78:37).

Similarly, the constancy of God is described by means of a complementary vocabulary. God "remembered that they were but flesh" (78:39); "is mindful of his covenant forever" (105:8); "he remembered his holy promise, / and Abraham, his servant" (105:42); "Nevertheless he regarded their distress / when he heard their cry. / For their sake he remembered his covenant / and showed compassion according to the abundance of his steadfast love" (106:44-45); and "being compassionate, / [God] forgave their iniquity . . . / he restrained his anger" (78:38).

Some significant theological implications emerge from this brief survey of the historical material in the Psalms. First, while the material acknowledges that compassion, mercy, and fidelity are aspects of God's nature (cf. 78:38; 106:45), the point emphasized is that *God's faithfulness is in service of God's relationship with Israel.* Over and over, these psalms stress that it was because of God's relational commitments—God's promises, holy words, covenants— that God proved faithful. God "remembered his holy promise," the psalms say. Or "God was mindful of his covenant." Having *established* the relationship with Israel by means of his *electing word*, God *sustains* the relationship by means of his fidelity. The commitment

God made to Abraham, Isaac, Joseph, Moses, and David led God to dispense with anger and punishment. God's commitment to those with whom God is in relationship is underscored even more strongly in a couple of places. Psalm 78 confesses that God "remembered that they were but flesh" (v. 39), and Psalm 106 says, God "regarded their distress" (v. 44), while Psalm 107 repeats that the Lord heard the cry of their voices in distress and concludes that God is moved to act when the people "are diminished and brought low / through oppression, trouble, and sorrow" (v. 39). These passages bear witness to a God whose sheer commitment to the creatures he has chosen to be in relationship with moves God to be faithful. The material suggests that for no other reason than God's care for those with whom he is in relationship—simply because God knows "that they are flesh"—God is faithful.

To confess God as faithful, however, does not mean that God never punishes or grows angry. And these psalms do repeatedly speak of God's anger as part of the relational and covenantal matrix. God's anger, however, serves the relationship God has with the people; it does not end it. As Psalm 78 says, "The anger of God rose against them . . . / and laid low the flower of Israel . . . / they repented and sought God earnestly" (vv. 31, 34). And Psalm 89 says of the Davidic monarchs, "I will punish their transgression with the rod . . . / but I will not remove from him my steadfast love" (vv. 32-33). Two points should be stressed. First, God's anger, too, is relational. It is not a random, capricious emotion. It does not erupt of its own accord, like a volcano that (from a human perspective) may seem to spew forth with no warning or precipitating cause. Rather, God's anger must be provoked by human infidelity. It flashes forth as a relational response to human sin. God's anger is not permanent; it rises in response to evil deeds done either to God's people or by God's people. Second, God's anger is not the opposite of God's faithfulness, but one aspect of God's faithfulness. Because God is faithful to those with whom he is in relationship, it burns forth against those who cause suffering: "When they are diminished and brought low," Psalm 107 says, "he pours contempt on princes" (vv. 39-40). Moreover, when God's anger is kindled against God's own people, and once the people are driven to repent, then God's faithfulness is shown in forgiveness (78:38; more on this below).

The Psalmists' Expectations of God's Faithfulness

Public confessions about God inevitably lead to populations (publics) with expectations regarding God. And from the texts of the Psalms, it is clear that Israel's confession "The Lord is faithful" led Israel to develop a set of expectations about what the Lord's fidelity would or ought to look like. In order to explore the expectations that ancient Israelites developed in response to the confession that the Lord is faithful, one can explore the lament psalms and examine what the psalmists expect in light of God's fidelity. One can also search the trust psalms for causal linkages between God's fidelity and specific actions or circumstances. When we study these verses, we find that the psalmists connect the confession of the Lord's faithfulness with specific manifestations. A partial list of these manifestations includes:

Protection from enemies (implied also is judgment of the wicked):

> You are indeed my rock and my fortress;
>> for your name's sake lead me and guide me,
> take me out of the net that is hidden for me,
>> for you are my refuge. (31:3-4)

> But you, O Lord, are a shield around me,
>> my glory, and the one who lifts up my head. (3:3)

> God is my shield,
>> who saves the upright in heart. (7:10)

Guidance through life:

> The Lord will keep you from all evil;
>> he will keep your life.

The LORD will keep
>your going out and your coming in
>from this time on and forevermore. (121:7-8)

Good and upright is the LORD;
>therefore he instructs sinners in the way.
He leads the humble in what is right,
>and teaches the humble his way.
All the paths of the LORD are steadfast love and faithfulness,
>for those who keep his covenant and his decrees. (25:8-10)

Deliverance from crisis (such as hunger, disease, natural disaster):

Your steadfast love, O LORD, extends to the heavens,
>your faithfulness to the clouds.
Your righteousness is like the mighty mountains,
>your judgments are like the great deep;
>you save humans and animals alike, O LORD. (36:5-6)

In you our ancestors trusted;
>they trusted, and you delivered them. (22:4)

Answer to prayer:

But as for me, my prayer is to you, O LORD.
>At an acceptable time, O God,
>in the abundance of your steadfast love, answer me.
With your faithful help rescue me
. . . .
Answer me, O LORD, for your steadfast love is good;
>according to your abundant mercy, turn to me. (69:13-14,
>>16)

I call upon you, for you will answer me, O God;
>incline your ear to me, hear my words.
Wondrously show your steadfast love,
>O savior of those who seek refuge
>from their adversaries at your right hand. (17:6-7)

Justice when falsely accused:

> Vindicate me, O Lord, my God,
>> according to your righteousness,
>> and do not let them rejoice over me. (35:24)

Forgiveness of sins:

> Have mercy on me, O God,
>> according to your steadfast love;
> according to your abundant mercy
>> blot out my transgressions. (51:1)

> If you, O Lord, should mark iniquities,
>> Lord, who could stand?
> But there is forgiveness with you, so that you may be revered.
> . . . .
> O Israel, hope in the Lord!
>> For with the Lord there is steadfast love,
>> and with him is great power to redeem. (130: 3-4, 7)

Food and provision from creation:

> May those who sow in tears
>> reap with shouts of joy.
> Those who go out weeping,
>> bearing the seed for sowing,
> shall come home with shouts of joy,
>> carrying their sheaves. (126:5-6)

The keeping of God's promises:

> Let your steadfast love come to me, O Lord,
>> your salvation according to your promise. (119:41)

> I bow down towards your holy temple
>> and give thanks to your name for your steadfast love and
>>> your faithfulness;
>> for you have exalted your name and your word above every-
>>> thing. (138:2)

The theological expectations that populations of believers develop in response to public confessions about God are often problematic because these expectations are often understood by those believers as normative. That is, Israel's ancient believers may have expected the "benefits" (103:1) of the divine-human covenant relationship to be mechanistically available. The suffering that life inevitably brings to all people would naturally result, therefore, in experiences of questioning the Lord's fidelity.

Experiences of Suffering That Call God's Fidelity into Question

The above list of expectations offers a sketch of what Israel expected the benefits of God's fidelity to be. As a result of this world-view, individual psalmists who experienced the opposite of these things—disease, hunger, illness, injury, false accusation, disability and the like—called out to God and community for vindication. In the individual psalms of lament, the sufferers often describe their physical suffering. The extended complaints in Psalms 22 and 38 can serve as examples of loss of health and of bodily suffering in the Psalms. The sufferer in Psalm 22 complains:

> I am poured out like water,
>   and all my bones are out of joint;
> my heart is like wax;
>   it is melted within my breast;
> my mouth is dried up like a potsherd,
>   and my tongue sticks to my jaws;
> . . . .
> My hands and feet have shriveled;
> I can count all my bones. (14-17)

Similarly, in Psalm 38 the psalmist cries out:

> There is no soundness in my flesh
>   because of your indignation;

there is no health in my bones
   because of my sin.
. . . .
My wounds grow foul and fester
   because of my foolishness;
I am utterly bowed down and prostrate;
   all day long I go around mourning.
For my loins are filled with burning,
   and there is no soundness in my flesh.
I am utterly spent and crushed;
. . . .
My heart throbs, my strength fails me;
   as for the light of my eyes—it also has gone from me.
. . . .
But I am like the deaf, I do not hear;
   like the mute, who cannot speak. (vv. 3-13)

The language of bodily suffering in these and others psalms can be, and often has been, taken metaphorically by interpreters. Peter Craigie, for example, comments regarding Psalm 22, "The words of vv. 15-16 should not necessarily be taken as indicative of . . . disease as such, rather, they describe the fear evoked by the enemies who are waiting and watching for death to come."[12] Or again, commenting on Psalm 31, "it is difficult to know whether the terminology should be interpreted literally or metaphorically."[13] And in a canonical sense, it is appropriate that these psalms have been prayed by people in many generations suffering from a variety of physical, spiritual, and emotional maladies. But it is equally appropriate to take these descriptions quite literally and to explore the theological questions, hopes, and confessions of those ancient psalmists who cried to God, "My strength fails . . . / my bones waste away" (31:10). That is the approach I am pursuing here, proceeding on the assumption that much of the psalmists' complaints about bodily suffering reflect genuine physical illness, loss of ability, injury, or pain.

Although the richly metaphorical language of the Psalms can be difficult to pin down, in general it seems that there is a variety of types of physical suffering about which the psalmists complain. They suffer from disease—"my eyes waste away" (6:7, see also 31:10).[14] They suffer from the physical decline brought on by old age (Psalm 71). They suffer from wounds, either inflicted by or exacerbated by enemies—"With a deadly wound in my body, my adversaries taunt me" (42:10; cf. 62:4; 94:6). They even suffer from suffering—"I am weary with my crying; my throat is parched" (69:3); "my knees are weak through fasting" (109:24); "I am too wasted to eat my bread, / because of my loud groaning / my bones cling to my skin" (102:4-5). The most important aspect to note about these ailments, however, is that the suffering is real—and that this suffering causes the psalmists paradoxically to question God's fidelity and to turn to God for deliverance.

The causes of these physical ailments are also diverse. Some are caused (or at least believed to have been caused by) the psalmists themselves—either by sin or by their own errors. Some are caused by or are exacerbated by the enemies. Some are caused by God—either as a punishment for sin or as a result of simply living within a fallen and random creation, in which accidents happen and people grow old and die (cf. Psalm 90). The most important aspect to note about the various causes of the psalmists' suffering is this—that no matter what the proximate cause of suffering, for the psalmists, God is in it somewhere. Even where the psalmists repent of and assume responsibility for sin, they nevertheless demand that God's anger be turned away. Even where enemies are the cause of suffering, the psalmists paradoxically also charge God. That is, the enemies are the agents of the psalmists' suffering, and for this they are guilty; simultaneously, the Lord is an agent of the psalmists' suffering and responsible for deliverance.

The crises that the psalmists experienced were intensified by accompanying theological crises—the experience of suffering led to an existential questioning of God's fidelity. This existential questioning took shape in several dimensions.

The first dimension of this questioning is a lack of confidence in God's fidelity within the created order. Above, I explored the

Psalter's confession that creation is one realm in which God's fidelity is experienced. But when the discernible order of creation appears to be broken in the sense of being disrupted or when the discernible order of creation appears to be malfunctioning or unjust—then the ordering of creation becomes not a basis for trusting in the Lord's faithfulness but a basis for distrust. Again, it cannot be doubted that many people experience their own suffering or the suffering of another as a sign that the orders of creation are broken, becoming for some a reason for challenging the confession that the Lord is faithful. The experiences of birth defects, disease, accidentally caused disability, and the like all call into question the idea that creation is trustworthy.

Another dimension of the psalmists' theological crisis is experienced in the mismanagement of creation's hierarchical order by those in places of power. The Psalms testify that God's fidelity in creation is experienced in its hierarchical arrangement. Above, I argued that, according to the Psalter, when the creatively endowed hierarchies fashioned into creation operate smoothly, creation mirrors the faithful character of God. Conversely, however, the texts of the many lament psalms force any reflective interpreter to admit that this ideal case is often not reflected in how those in positions of power and responsibility carry out their tasks. Parents are often negligent or abusive. Those in positions of power in both governmental and religious institutions are often either incompetent or corrupt. Humanity as a whole is on its way to earning a low grade in her task of exercising servant dominion over God's creation. Thus, in most of the psalms of lament, the psalmists complain of those who have power—of the wicked, the unrighteous, the sinners—and how their misuse of their hierarchically derived power is in direct contrast to the faithful and trustworthy world that the Lord has promised.

A third dimension of the psalmists' theological crisis is located in their experience that the people of God—the community of faith that exists to be a countertestimony to the world's infidelity and a means of faithfulness for the individual sufferer—this very community exacerbates suffering rather than ameliorates it. That is, rather than serving as a channel through which God's fidelity is manifest, they dam up God's fidelity and hold it back from becoming incarnate. Thus, the psalmist of Psalm 41 complains, "Even my bosom friend in whom I trusted, / who ate of my bread, has lifted the heel against me" (v. 41:9). And the priestly author of Psalm 55 complains of a fellow priest, "my equal, / my companion, my familiar friend" with whom he once "kept pleasant company [and] walked in the house of God with the throng" has "violated a covenant with me" (vv. 13-14, 20). The experience of these psalmists, mirrored so often still today in the way that the disabled are excluded from communities of faith, is perhaps part of the reason why the disabled are the most unchurched population in our society. In addition to the physical suffering they experience, they also experience isolation from God's community—the community at times expels them, cannot negotiate a way to include them.

A fourth dimension of the theological crisis of the psalmists is the dimension of being accused of sin. In the ancient world and still often in the modern world, the assumption is that when a person suffers, they have caused it themselves—either by having sinned, by having exercised poor judgment, or by having made a mistake. The psalmists were often accused of having caused their own suffering. Thus the psalmist of Psalm 4, perhaps having been falsely accused, asserts his or her "right" (= "just cause"; Hebrew ṣedeq) and asks God to be gracious. The accusations of sins are "lies" (v. 2). And so often the psalmists assert their innocence. These assertions of innocence question, therefore, not only the fidelity of the community and its justice system but the trustworthiness of the Lord, who has called the community into being.

Means of God's Faithfulness

It is important to note that while the Psalter does not stifle the protests of the lament psalms or the questions that these psalms raise about God's fidelity, it nevertheless persists in its central witness that the Lord is faithful. The sufferers in the psalms do not rush to resolve the theological dissonance that their experiences of suffering create. On the one hand, they do not silence the challenge to God—as do Job's friends do by asserting that Job must have sinned or as the wicked in the Psalter do who assume that disability is a sign of God's disfavor. On the other hand, they do not silence the predominant testimony that God is faithful—as the enemies do in the Psalter, who assert that "God does not see" or who mock, "Where is your God?" Rather, singing a song of resistance and pain, the sufferers base their appeals to God precisely on the discordant contrast between the promise that God is faithful and the experiences of suffering, which seem to belie that confession. And often, the psalmists move out of those low moments, so that they are again able to confess that the Lord is faithful.

The communal memory of and witness to God's faithfulness plays a major role in the way the Psalter holds together both the questions of ancient believers regarding the fidelity of the Lord, on the one hand, and the central witness that "the steadfast love of the Lord endures forever, and his faithfulness to all generations," on the other. Neck deep in the flood, the psalmists remember God's faithful deeds in the past—"In you our ancestors trusted; / they trusted, and you delivered them" (22:4); "These things I remember, / as I pour out my soul; / how I went with the throng, / and led them in procession to the house of God" (42:4). Experiencing in these memories both a torturous reminder of how much better things could be and also a comforting reminder that God has done great things in the past, the psalmists sit down to wait for the Lord (40:1).

Indeed, the Psalter pushes on to name at least three "means" through which God's fidelity is made available to Israel and the world. These three means are the Davidic king, the city of Jerusalem, and the people of God.

The King

First, the king. One of the most difficult aspects of theological witness of the Psalms for modern readers to grasp—especially

Christian readers of the Psalms—is the Psalter's understanding of the king as a means of God's faithfulness. In other Old Testament traditions, notably in the Deuteronomistic History and the Major Prophets, the attitude toward the monarchy ranges somewhere between conflicted ambivalence and concerned suspicion.[15] The Psalter betrays little evidence of this conflictedness regarding the monarchy. It portrays the monarchy as almost pure blessing.[16] The language of God's fidelity is ascribed both to the king as an instrument of God and as the person with whom God is paradigmatically in relationship. Psalm 45 uses confessional language regarding the king that is elsewhere reserved for God:

> Your throne, O God, endures for ever and ever.
>> Your royal scepter is a scepter of equity;
>> you love righteousness and hate wickedness.
> Therefore God, your God, has anointed you
>> with the oil of gladness beyond your companions. (vv. 6-7)

And Psalm 72 prays for the king to fulfill the promise of the office in such a fashion as to embody God's reign:

> Give the king your justice, O God,
>> and your righteousness to a king's son.
> May he judge your people with righteousness,
>> and your poor with justice.
> May the mountains yield prosperity for the people,
>> and the hills, in righteousness.
> May he defend the cause of the poor of the people,
>> give deliverance to the needy,
>> and crush the oppressor. (vv. 1-4)[17]

The City

Second, in a largely similar fashion, the Psalms celebrate Zion as a means of God's faithfulness. The term Zion encompasses the temple, the holy mount, and the city of Jerusalem. The Psalms apply theological language to Zion/Jerusalem that elsewhere is reserved for God. The city is "his habitation" (132:13), "my holy hill" (2:6;

cf. 15:1); "the hill of the LORD . . . his holy place" (24:3), "the city of God, / the holy habitation of the Most High" (46:4), "the joy of all the earth" (48:2), "your dwelling place" (84:1), "the house of the LORD" (122:1), and the like. Psalm 48 goes so far as to call the city itself "God":

> Walk about Zion, go all around it,
> > count its towers,
> consider well its ramparts;
> > go through its citadels,
> that you may tell the next generation
> > that this is God,
> our God for ever and ever.
> > He will be our guide for ever. (vv. 12-14)

The city is seen as the manifestation of God's faithfulness, with the Psalms confessing that the city delivers God's steadfast love and faithfulness: "We ponder your steadfast love, O God, / in the midst of your temple" (48:9).

The People of God

The third means of God's faithfulness confessed in the Psalter is the people of God. The very concept of the people as "God's people" is a relational concept—that the people are a people defined by their relationship with God. As Hans-Joachim Kraus has written, "The only way that Yahweh is known is in relationships—Yahweh is the God of Israel and Israel the people of Yahweh (Wellhausen)."[18] Throughout the Psalms, those who suffer alternately lament that the wicked make their suffering worse and plead with "the righteous" to lighten their load.[19] In the Psalms, "righteous" is not merely a moral term. As Jerome Creach has helpfully argued, the righteous are those who are dependent on God—"They recognize their sinfulness and pray for divine forgiveness; and they plead for deliverance from enemies."[20] To that I would add that throughout the Psalter the righteous are those who provide hospitality and community for others who are beleaguered and assaulted.[21]

Theological Implications

The Psalter's language that speaks of the king, the city, and the people as means through which the fidelity of God is mediated and communicated offers at least a provisional bridge over the chasm that might divide the confession that the Lord is faithful from the questions surrounding that confession. God's purposes are worked out through earthen vessels. This does not diminish God's agency, but it does qualify it. It means that God's agency is often a mediated faithfulness. It means that when drawing conclusions about God as the cause of events, one needs to be attentive to the reality that the Psalms describe God's work as work often mediated through other agents. It also means that one needs to be attentive to the fact that God's faithful actions and intentions are part of a larger web of fidelity. God's faithfulness has formed a trustworthy creation, with laws and orders that offer a trustworthy environment in which life can teem. But to a believer who falls from a high precipice and cries out to God for deliverance (one thinks here of Ps 91:12), God's fidelity to the law of gravity may not seem comforting. The anthropocentric narrowness with which the individual believer, or the individual community, or even the human species as a whole tends to approach the question of God's fidelity needs to be examined in light of the Psalter's witness to the broad range of God's fidelity. The human creature tends to reduce God's fidelity to a single relational strand connecting God and the believer (or the believer's community). The Psalter, however, seems to paint God's fidelity as a web of relational commitments, in which the Lord remains faithful not only to one individual or one community but to a dizzying array of creatures and creations.

Second, a distinction between the office of both the king and the city, on the one hand, and the individual human kings and human residents of the city, on the other, is helpful in terms of unpacking the Psalter's witness to the Lord's faithfulness. To the extent that the Psalter affirms that king as a means of God's faithfulness, it is affirming the office and the vocation rather than the individuals who mostly failed to live up to the ideal the biblical witness imagines. Similar to the New Testament confession in which governing authorities are a gift from God and those who resist governing offices are resisting God (Romans 13) but can also express great resistance and criticism of those authorities (Revelation), the Psalms see the office of king as a channel of God's activity, but not one that is beyond fault.[22] Similarly, cities are often dangerous places, made of up communities of sinners. But the city has an office in as much as the city is the habitation of God, meaning that it is also the means through which God's presence is mediated. This is the case for two reasons. First, because the city is a place of order. As the Psalms confess the orderly and trustworthy creation that God has fashioned as a realm of God's fidelity, so the city of God is seen as a means of God's faithfulness in that it mediates order; and through it God is fashioning a trustworthy and ordered realm in which human beings may live. Thus, the singer of Psalm 101, who is likely the Davidic king, commits himself to looking "with favor on the faithful in the land, / so that they may live with me" but also vows that "no one who practices deceit shall remain in my house" and that he will cut "off all evildoers from the city of the LORD" (vv. 6-8). Second, the city is a means of grace because it is the solely authorized site of worship. Part and parcel with Zion as a means of faithfulness is that the city is the site of the temple, not only God's habitation, but also of the site of temple worship and thus the source of all the blessings that come to the people through worship. Among these blessings are forgiveness (Psalm 51), the simple act of "blessing" that I take to mean the bestowal of favorable conditions on the people (Psalm 134), "justice" (Psalm 99), restoration to community (Ps 70:4-5), "rest" (cf. 95:11), fertility for the land (Psalm 42/43), and even the threatening, rebuking presence of God (Psalms 50, 81, 95).

Third, the Psalter affirms God as an active agent in the world not in spite of but precisely because of the mediated nature of God's activity. In the Psalms, so often the wicked and the unrighteous assert that God "does not see"—that God is not an active agent. The

Psalter offers the counterconfession that God is an active agent in the world. It confesses that although this fidelity is mediated by the king or city or people or creation, it is nevertheless God's fidelity. Just to take the example of the community of God at worship, the Psalter confesses that Israel is not the chief actor in worship, God is. It is surely no accident that no complete ritual texts or instructions survive in the Psalter. The Psalter underemphasizes the ritual observations of the people both by ignoring ritual instructions and by disparaging Israel's rites (cf. Pss 50:12-15; 51:16). The Psalter's emphasis on God's desiring "sacrifices of thanksgiving" rather than "the flesh of bulls" (51:13-14) is not only a witness to the sort of worship that God desires but also a witness to the confession that God is the one who acts in worship. The act of thanksgiving is *not something that the worshiper does on behalf of God* but is rather testimony to the human congregation that *it is God who has acted in God's characteristically faithful fashion.* As Psalm 40 bears witness,

> I have told the glad news of deliverance
>   in the great congregation;
> . . . .
> I have not hidden your saving help within my heart,
>   I have spoken of your faithfulness and your salvation;
> I have not concealed your steadfast love and your faithfulness
>   from the great congregation. (vv. 9-10)

CHAPTER 8

Rethinking the Enterprise: What Must Be Considered in Formulating a Theology of the Psalms

Beth Tanner

About the time I began to write this essay, my son was play-ing a computer game in which the purpose is to find hidden objects. He had found every object except a bat. To fully understand this story, you should know that much of my son's ten-year-old life is taken up by baseball. He lives and breathes the game. Baseball colors his perspective on the world. So he searched and searched for that bat hidden in the picture. Then my daughter walked by and said, "Hey, the bat is easy to find; it is hanging right there in the tree." Sure enough, when he looked with a different frame of reference, there was a fuzzy brown bat hanging upside down from the tree. He had forgotten that a bat can be an implement of the game or the nickname of a mammal. His context defined what he searched for and prevented him from seeing other possibilities. The same can be said for theological work in the Psalms; we can only find what our own context has structured and trained us to see.

The open acknowledgment of this reality and an understand-ing of how it colors our interpretations has changed the way we go about the task of biblical theology in recent years. Previously, objec-tive study held center stage. Theology was about finding univer-sals that were based on Western paradigms of logic, rationality, and sequential thinking. The point was to discover the truth through objective investigation of the biblical texts. Unfortunately, this truth and the way to discern it was debated for over two hundred years by those interested in creating a biblical theology.[1]

When this quest was abandoned, the next major focus was to search for a center or *Mitte*, but this quest too led to more arguments about the shape of that center.[2] Biblical theology needed a new direction, one that took into account the issue of contexts, both ancient and modern. It needed to become a discipline that talked about ways of knowing instead of looking for an objective way to identify a truth or a center. Biblical theology needed to evolve, and in the past few years, scholars have been wrestling with that evolution and asking new questions. These questions are important to this volume because, before one can engage in a "theology of the Psalms," one needs to understand what it means to "do" theology in a multicultural, multivoiced world.

How does one, then, "do" theology in the twenty-first century? Theology is a human enterprise. It is "God-talk." Erhard Gerstenberger comments on what the process means today:

> Theology can hardly be uniform, universal, and valid through the ages. Rather God-talk, for deeply divine and human reasons, for the very heart of faith must be contextual, temporary, unfinished and in a certain concordance with changing customs, cultures, and social conditions. Our theological discourse must not be taken as eternal truth. We think and talk as transitory beings, firmly tied to the textures of our socialization and cultural identities.[3]

Theology, then, is a contemporary enterprise, which necessitates that it also be a canonical enterprise.[4] The psalms we have are in the order, shape, and texture that are contained in the current books of Psalms.[5] A psalm's meaning is embedded in its place within a particular book, a book with poem-prayers in a particular order.[6] This does not mean that a theology of the Psalms written today is not in conversation with and even influenced by both what is known about the ancient cult and the people as well as the interpretation of the Psalms over the centuries. These other interpretations from across the centuries can inform us in our quest, but the meaning of the Psalms today is in this moment, in the post-Holocaust, post-9/11, fear-driven, economically dicey, global-economy world. This theology is not the same one the ancients would have voiced and must never be confused with it. In addition, we may share some of our worldview with the folks interpreting the Psalms fifty years ago, but their view cannot be seen as equivalent to ours. This basic point is often overlooked in academic settings, and we often write from a perspective that appears universal. We must, however, for the sake of clear understanding, speak of the temporal nature of our work if for no other reason than to remind ourselves and the readers that the present worldview and the worldview of these biblical poems or even our grandparents cannot be thought of as one in the same.

One simple example will illustrate this point. In the United States immediately after World War II, psalms of lament held some interest for scholars, but in the literature and liturgy of the church, lament and its demanding style of prayer had all but disappeared. Walter Brueggemann's 1986 article "The Costly Loss of Lament" fell mostly on the deaf ears of a church humming a positivistic theology.[7] However, in a post-9/11 world, the literature about lament in both scholarship and the church has exploded.[8] Our experience has shaped our canon within a canon.

This idea is especially salient when the subject of study is poetry. Poetry, to be effective, must be deeply contextual. This contemporary focus on the lament genre did not come from some new cult-functional discovery in the ancient text but from our own sorrow and pain and the very present need for the church to address the situation. Our post-9/11 cultural concerns set the agenda. Those ancient cries of sorrow were just waiting there in the Psalter until we needed their words to help us express our own hurt, sorrow, and anger in our own lives. We found words that expressed our emotions, but this rediscovery of the lament psalms does not mean that everything between us and the ancients has collapsed. We can meet each other on a emotional level, but the situation that caused the pain remains bound to its own contextual matrix.

Brueggemann adds additional definition to the task of theology. He writes:

> What counts is a *pluralistic* interpretive community that permits us to see the polymorphic character of the text, and the *deprivileged* circumstance whereby theological interpretation in a Christian context is no longer allied with or supported by the dominant epistemological or political-ideological forces. . . . Or more briefly, hermeneutical problematics and possibilities have now displaced positivistic claims—historical and theological—as the matrix of theological reflections.[9]

Brueggemann's evaluation of the state of theology certainly moves beyond a single center or even a single metaphor. Singularity is a relic of the past when The One Truth, or center, was the dominant cultural norm. What we know now is that a singular way of truth-telling included only those of certain races, genders, and nationalities. We are now moving toward an interpretive community of voices in conversation instead of competition. It is only with a variety of voices that we have a chance to explore the richness of the poetry of the Psalms.

To summarize, at the beginning of the twenty-first century, the biblical theological enterprise has become *contextual and thus canonical, transitory, and pluralistic.* Meaning cannot be discovered by objective investigation of what was, either in the ancient world or in the full history of interpretation; yet this knowledge must inform and enrich any work in biblical theology, which is a constant conversation that broadens horizons and confronts our view of the world and culture with the poems and stories of the biblical text. It is with this understanding of biblical theology in general that we turn now to look at what the Psalms are and how they function both as poetry and as theological matrix.

First and foremost, the Psalms are poetry. In the past, under the careful eye of Western rationalism, this simple and obvious point was ignored. Poetry was eclipsed by historical and rational pursuits as historical criticism became the gold standard of biblical study. Poetry, with its rich metaphors and limited historical references, became a lesser genre to the narratives, with their plentiful historical information.[10] Under this historical framework, the cult-functional method became the primary way of studying psalms. As such, their poetic nature was eclipsed by how a song was used in cultic temple worship. The poetic nature of the words and metaphors was left to the composers of hymns as scholars searched for the essence of Israel's worship embedded in the genres of the Psalter.

Currently, however, the academy is becoming interested in the poetry that is the matrix of these texts. Psalms are sung poems and have a place in their own right as words that create, disturb, and comfort. Each is unique and is meant to be seen as a whole, not chopped into pieces with its parts reconstructed on the altar of theological or dogmatic themes.[11] Each psalm also has a distinctive place in the Psalter, and that too plays an additional role in its message. Any discussion of the theology of the Psalms can only occur by acknowledging and honoring each psalm's poetic function and its unique placement within the whole book of Psalms.

The second reason why the medium of poetry matters may surprise even a seasoned biblical scholar because it is biological, buried in our DNA itself. We are, it seems, created to process poetry differently than prose. Neurobiologists note that poetry and music are processed in what is usually the nondominant, right side of the brain, while narrative is processed by the analytical, dominant side of the brain.[12] Put simply, as biological machines, we use a different part of our brains when we encounter poetry and music. Music and poetry memory banks are also either processed or stored in different parts of the brain than rational day-to-day cognitive thought. This is clearly seen with stroke, dementia, or Alzheimer's patients, who can often sing songs long after they lose the ability to perform day-to-day tasks. Scientists and doctors have documented this phenomenon, and now music and singing are part of the therapy for Alzheimer's patients.[13] Poetry, especially poetry set to music, speaks to us in places that prose does not. It offers a change from the everyday. It has a staying power, even in minds damaged by disease. The question for the theologian then is how should this biological fact influence our work? This area needs much more research, but if poetry functions differently in the brain, should its theology engage the opposite, more analytical side, or should the theology spoken out of the Psalms remain in the poetic realm alone? A discussion of the theology of the Psalms should, on some level, grapple with this very question.

The third point about poetry returns to one of the points made about biblical theology in general. Poetry, with its rich metaphors and word pictures, is uniquely contextual, and this is both good and bad news for modern interpreters. It is bad news because we cannot transport ourselves back to understand the depth and breadth of the riches of these words in their time and place. There will be metaphors and sections of these poems that elude us both because of differing contexts and because they are ancient hand-copied documents. We must tread carefully and responsibly. There is only a limited amount that we can know about how poetry functioned in ancient cultures. We can analyze the structures, metaphors, gaps, and ellipses, but as far as how poetry affected ancient people on a sociological level, the poetry is almost as mute as archaeological artifacts. One of the foundational understandings of the theological enterprise must be a recognition that there are many things about how poetry functioned in ancient cultures that we simply cannot access, and part of this new theological landscape is to admit where our knowledge is less than we would hope. Chances are we will never recover how the Psalms were used in the cult, and if that is true, then we can certainly know even less about how the poetry formed the society as a whole and the faith and worship life of individuals. We must be willing to say there are things that we do not understand about the interaction of this poetry and our ancient ancestors, and there are also parts of the Psalms where meaning is as elusive as a puff of smoke.

There is also good news in these poetic texts, for the fourth point is that the Psalms have a great capacity to reach the reader on an emotional level, a biological function that has remained the same in humans throughout time. As Patrick Miller has noted, the Psalms are not completely bound by either their historical context or even by much of their content.[14] The ancients may not have had the same context and worldview as we do, but through the centuries all have understood the words, "My God, My God, Why have you forsaken me?" and "Happy are those whose transgression is lifted!" The Psalms as poems describe human emotion in such vivid terms that the connection is automatic. The ancients did not know the context of modern joys and sorrows—many of these would have been alien to them—but the emotions that these events produce are embedded in their laments and can now be used to voice our cries and praises to God in the present.

So doing theology in the Psalms is transitory, pluralistic, and requires reminding ourselves that what we see and hear is vastly different from those of our ancient ancestors, and we cannot ignore the differences between the two cultures. The Psalms reach places in both the brain and the heart that other genres do not.

So if theology of the Psalms is transitory, pluralistic, and incomplete, and our brains process them differently from rational thought, what else must be added to the list for our work in the poetry of the Psalms? Gerald Wilson described the Psalms this way: "In them royal ideology and prophetic critique, cultic theology and wisdom reflection, law and liturgy all collide and intertwine to create a complex yet piquant stew of biblical proportions."[15] In other words, the Psalms as a whole are as diverse, divergent, contrasting, and comforting as our lives and our relationships! Just as in theology in general, to do justice to the Psalms means to reflect not a smooth center or one meaning but to somehow capture the complex whole. This certainly makes the presentation messier, but to do otherwise is to offer a reduced truth. It is not just the modern interpretation that is complex; it is the Psalms themselves, and we must acknowledge and capture in any way that we can the scope of their emotional landscape in all of its variegated terrain.

The next element crucial to any theological work on the Psalms has been named by Brueggemann as "hermeneutical problems and possibilities" and by Wilson as "unresolved tension." This is where the issue of "gaps" comes in. In other publications, I have argued that gaps should be a recognized term in the syntax of Hebrew poetry. Meir Sternberg argues that gaps are a part of all of literature and require decisions by the reader/hearer in order to make sense of the text.[16] Gaps can be small and easy to traverse or, as Sternberg notes, may be an arduous task, where the reader must work "consciously, laboriously, hesitantly, and with constant modifications" to make sense of the text.[17] Gaps either within individual psalms or between psalms that have been placed next to each other are not mistakes or happenstance but are indeed part of the character of poetry itself. The Psalms testify to the fact that tension is not something that, at the end of the day, can be fixed easily; and these gaps and tensions, as part of the very structure of psalms and the Psalter, argue against consensus and easy answers. Wilson echoes this in his own work, "The life of the psalms is a messy life where pain and joy, self-knowledge and self-doubt, love and hatred, trust and suspicion break in upon one another, overlapping and competing for our attention."[18] Any theological presentation of the Psalms must have room for—or better yet, openly name—tension, even unresolved tension, as part of its structure.

The gaps and their tension bring forth another reality about these poems: not only do they engage the nondominant, or creative, side of our brains; they also place a strain on the dominant or rational side of the brain. The two sides must work to bridge the gaps, understand the metaphors, and engage the images. Reading or listening to poetry is work—brain work. It requires us to access our memories and bring together feelings, words, and stored images. Each interaction is a new creation of mind and word. In the work of poetry, one struggles to understand and bring life to the word pictures. Poetry, then, is an untamed medium, for its interaction with each person is different. No matter how I try, I cannot capture all of the possibilities when poetry meets the human mind and spirit. So when speaking of the theology of the Psalms, we need to take into account this aspect, for like the others, it is a part of how these poetic prayers function. Our ventures into the Psalms must be as open and engaging of the mind and spirit as these poems, or again, we reduce the very purpose of the medium.

In addition, each prayer-poem can function differently based on the immediate context of the one reading or hearing it. A psalm of praise or trust can have the texture of smooth glass one day, yet another day when life is hard and God seems distant that very same psalm can feel like the rough texture of a storm-tossed sea. The words on the page are not where this interaction happens. It happens in the heart and, yes, both sides of the brain in the one encountering the poem. The place of theological expression is within us. Again for some, this may seem obvious. But for so many years, we have held the Psalms at arm's length, pretending that their words and images affect some ancient psalmist and not us. The place of poetry is in us and is not external. To give justice to this psalmic poetry, we must speak of its power, not in the lives of ancient people or in the life of the nebulous psalmist, but in our own hearts and minds. The shape of the book itself testifies to this reality. Psalm 150, the last, the finale, is not a capstone song that closes the book but one that is all invitation, that opens up the Psalms. It is an invitation for the hearer or reader to continue what they have just experienced and add their own words to the words found there.

So a theology of the Psalms must be transitory, not only over a generation but over our own fleeting encounters with the poetry over time. It is also conversational, whether that conversation be with ourselves in how the Psalms feel different at different times in our lives or with persons from different cultural contexts who view the poetry through lives different from the ones we live. This theology should also reflect the diversity and tension inherent within the text of the Psalms and in our interactions with the poetry. Finally, a theology of the Psalms must be uncertain and tentative, for there are allusions that elude us and others as we change over the course of our lives and live out our faith in a contemporary context.

So, having said all of this, it would seem that we are in an impossibly complex matrix, in which a comprehensive or systematic way of speaking of the Psalms would do nothing more than reduce these poems to something less than what they are. Each interaction with either one or a series of these 150 poem-prayers offers a broad range of possibilities. Yet at the same time, the Psalms are a unique genre for theological reflection, for just like theology, they are God-talk. In a way other texts cannot, the Psalms are "a large collection of words uttered to God and about God, but not from God."[19] But again, one must tread carefully in how this is understood. They are God-talk, but they are not the random utterances of an individual or individuals. In a recent article, Carl Bosma made this point clear.[20] We may not know everything about the Psalms and the cult, but what we do know is that the Psalms were used in ancient worship, so they are meant to shape the faith of a people. In this, they are much more than individual prayers, for as individual psalms or psalm groups and as a whole book, the Psalms tell us about the complex picture that these ancients had of God. The Psalms, then, are more than a book of individual prayers; they are a way to shape faith and belief in a poetic form that makes the brain work in ways different from our day-to-day routines.

Is there a place to at least start working at a theology of the Psalms? What I propose is not so much a defining of the center and or centers but to probe around the edges. I assign the same exercise to each person in the Psalms courses I teach both in the seminary and in churches. As part of their reflections, I ask students to explore this question: Why did the ancient people name this book *Tellehim*, or praises? When the collection was set and it was all said and done, they saw these poems as praise. This was not a title retained by the early Christian church, which changed the title to "songs." I said earlier that we can never know how the Psalms functioned sociologically, but in exploring this one question, we may gain insight into their thinking and at the same time probe our own understanding not only of individual psalms but of the collection as a whole. What I have discovered with this exercise is that the answers are easy and simplistic at the beginning when Psalms like 23 and 100 come to mind. But there is a lot of silence in the room when students are asked to explore why the ancients saw Psalms 88 and 109 as praise. As the class goes on, the reflections of all of us become more complex and tentative and individual as we struggle with the framing question. For myself, I know that I change and deepen my experience with the poetry every time I engage the question.

In closing, I will simply offer some of the discoveries of my students around this question. By the end of the term, most of them articulate the idea that the Psalter is praise because in all of the diversity, tension, and complexity of the Psalms, the conversation, no matter how difficult, goes on. It is praise, they say, because it reflects a real, deep, and lifelong relationship with God. I will add to their words that for me the Psalms are part of the biblical definition of Israel's name, meaning to strive with God. In addition, when one adds the shape of the book of Psalms to the question, it is clear that the Psalms move from lament to praise, so that, at the end, all other language has fallen away. The shape of the Psalms sheds all other human language in its journey from beginning to end until it reaches Psalm 150, which is not a praise psalm at all but a call to praise that invites all who have journeyed to this point to leave the words of others and engage in their own journeys of poetic verse that give the word pictures that define their own relationship with God.

So at the end of the day, the Psalms leave me, and I hope others, with not an answer but a question, a question that I think takes a lifetime to attempt to answer: What exactly constitutes "praise"? What I do know is that the answer is ever changing, partial, and cannot be collapsed into neat categories. It is conversational and is never fully captured in my or anyone else's words. In this, it reflects the vast, complex nature of God and reminds us that God, even with all of our theological jargon, is still a mystery we cannot quite capture. It also reflects a long life lived with that God, where the relationship depicted is deep, vast, complex, and sometimes full of contradiction. It shapes our faith because these psalms know us on an emotional level, tapping parts of the brain that other texts cannot access. The Psalms engage our whole self, and in that they offer a description of what these ancients meant by *nepeš* ("soul" or "life"). These poems are a gift that gives us a way to understand, grapple with, and grow in relationship with God and others. The answer may seem messy and unsatisfying to some, but it is this peculiar nature of their poetic edges that makes them so theological and pedagogically important.

Abbreviations

BZAW	Beihefte zur Zeitschrift für die alttestamentliche Wissenschaft
CBQ	*Catholic Biblical Quarterly*
FOTL	Forms of the Old Testament Literature
FRLANT	Forschungen zur Religion und Literatur des Alten und Neuen Testaments
HBT	*Horizons in Biblical Theology*
HUCA	*Hebrew Union College Annual*
Int	*Interpretation*
JAAR	*Journal of the American Academy of Religion*
JBL	*Journal of Biblical Literature*
JBS	*Journal of Biblical Studies*
JSOT	*Journal for the Study of the Old Testament*
JSOTSup	*Journal for the Study of the Old Testament: Supplement Series*
JTS	*Journal of Theological Studies*
MT	Masoretic Text
OBO	Orbis biblicus et orientalis
OTL	Old Testament Library
OTS	Old Testament Studies

SBLDS	Society of Biblical Literature Dissertation Series
SBLSymS	Society of Biblical Literature Symposium Series
SBM	Stuttgarter biblische Monographien
SJT	*Scottish Journal of Theology*
TBü	Theologische Bücherei
TDOT	*Theological Dictionary of the Old Testament*
TU	Texte und Untersuchungen
TZ	*Theologische Zeitschrift*
VTSup	Supplements to Vetus Testamentum
WMANT	Wissenschaftliche Monographien zum Alten und Neuen Testament
ZAW	*Zeitschrift für die alttestamentliche Wissenschaft*
ZTK	*Zeitschrift für Theologie und Kirche*

Notes

Preface

1. "Preface to the Psalter," in *Luther's Works* (trans. C. M. Jacobs and rev. E. T. Bachman; Philadelphia: Muhlenberg, 1960), 254.

Chapter 1: The Psalms and the Life of Faith

1. On the question of function and intentionality, see Hans Werner Hoffmann, "Form-Funktion-Intention," *ZAW* 82 (1970): 341–46; Kirsten Nielsen, *Yahweh as Prosecutor and Judge* (JSOTSup 9; Sheffield: Sheffield University Press, 1978), 1–4; and Rolf Knierim, "Old Testament Form Criticism Reconsidered," *Int* 27 (1973): 449–68. Much of the current discussion of function concerns the extent to which literary forms faithfully reflect and remain linked to their original setting and function. See especially Georg Fohrer, "Remarks on the Modern Interpretation of the Prophets," *JBL* 80 (1961): 309–19, and idem, "Tradition und Interpretation im Alten Testament," *ZAW* 32 (1961): 1–30, whom Hoffmann follows, and the more programmatic statement of Martin J. Buss, "The Study of Forms," in *Old Testament Form Criticism* (ed. John H. Hayes, Trinity University Monograph Series in Religion 2; San Antonio: Trinity University Press, 1974), 31–38.

2. Brevard S. Childs, "Midrash and the Old Testament," in *Understanding the Sacred Text* (ed. John Reumann; Valley Forge, Pa.: Judson, 1972), 51, understands the issue in this way: "One of the fundamental postulates

of the form-critical method is the insistence that the form and function of a genre must be held together. The attempt of the form-critical method to analyze the stereotyped form of a literary genre has the purpose of determining the sociological setting within the life of the community which by its recurrent pattern shaped the genre." In this statement Childs may hold the form and function more tightly together than does Fohrer. His statement is especially important because it is attentive to the sociology of both form and setting, a dimension too often ignored in form criticism. Reference to sociological reality affirms that in the use of the form, the community is doing something.

3. Ronald Clements, *A Century of Old Testament Study* (Philadelphia: Westminster Press, 1976), 79–95; Erhard Gerstenberger, "The Psalms," in *Old Testament Form Criticism* (ed. John H. Hayes, Trinity University Monograph Series in Religion 2; San Antonio: Trinity University Press, 1974), 198–221. In speaking of Gunkel's classification, Gerstenberger writes: "In general they still stand, or at least they can serve as a point of departure. The same holds true for form critical method" (187). "Gunkel's fourfold design of complaint psalms and thanksgiving songs still is fundamental to all discussion of the matter today" (198).

4. Claus Westermann, *The Praise of God in the Psalms* (Richmond: John Knox, 1965), 15–35, reprinted in *Praise and Lament in the Psalms* (Atlanta: John Knox, 1981).

5. Knierim, "Old Testament Form Criticism," has considerably broadened the question of *Sitz im Leben*, or the setting in life, away from its original focus on institutional origin, to show that setting concerned a variety of matrices, including language, mood, and style of an epoch. See also Douglas Knight, "The Understanding of 'Sitz im Leben' in Form Criticism," *SBL Seminar Papers* (Missoula, Mont.: Scholars, 1974), 105–25. Martin Buss, "The Idea of Sitz im Leben—History and Critique," *ZAW* 90 (1978): 157–70, has welcomed the new discussion broadly concerned with sociological context, but he has urged the use of other designations for sociological context so that it should not be confused with Gunkel's narrower, more precise meaning of the term.

6. On the hymn, see the suggestive hypothesis of Frank Crüsemann, *Zur Formgeschichte von Hymnus und Danklied in Israel* (WMANT 32; Neukirchen-Vluyn: Neukirchener Verlag, 1969). His proposal, however, appears to be too subtle and refines too much what can be determined by form. For a summary and evaluation of Mowinckel's dominant hypothesis, see the older statement of Aubrey Johnson, "The Psalms," in *The*

Old Testament and Modern Study (ed. H. H. Rowley; Oxford: Clarendon, 1951), 189–207, and more recently, Gerstenberger, "Psalms," 212–18, and Clements, *Century*, 83–95.

7. Westermann, *Praise of God*, 22.

8. The festival hypothesis has been given a full and comprehensive restatement by Aubrey Johnson, *The Cultic Prophet and Israel's Psalmody* (Cardiff: University of Wales Press, 1979).

9. Hans Schmidt, *Das Gebet der Angeklagten im Alten Testament* (BZAW 40; Giessen: Alfred Topelmann, 1928).

10. Walter Beyerlin, *Die Rettung der Bedrängten in den Feindpsalmen der Einzelnen auf institutionelle Zusammenhänge untersucht* (FRLANT 99; Göttingen: Vandenhoeck and Ruprecht, 1970). Lienhard Delekat, *Asylie und Schutzorakel am Zionheiligtum* (Leiden: E. J. Brill, 1967).

11. Erhard Gerstenberger, *Der bittende Mensch: Bittritual und Klagelied des Einzelnen im Alten Testament* (WMANT 51; Neukirchen-Vluyn: Neukirchener Verlag, 1980). See also Gerstenberger, "Der klagende Mensch," in *Probleme biblischer Theologie* (ed. Hans Walter Wolff; Munich: Christian Kaiser Verlag, 1971), 64–72.

12. In this connection, attention should be drawn to the important work of Rainer Albertz, *Weltschöpfung und Menschenschöpfung* (Calwer Theologische Monographien 3; Stuttgart: Calwer, 1974), and idem, *Persönliche Frömmigkeit und offizielle Religion* (Calwer Theologische Monographien 9; Stuttgart: Calwer, 1978), studies not unrelated to the proposals of Gerstenberger.

13. Knierim, "Old Testament Form Criticism," 466, links form-critical analysis to function. In general, form criticism is moving in the direction of sociology and anthropology. Thus, I would argue that, on the whole, the Psalms are concerned with the social construction and maintenance of reality. See Peter Berger and Thomas Luckmann, *The Social Construction of Reality* (Baltimore: Penguin, 1966). As one example of how this applies to the Psalms, see Walter Brueggemann, *The Psalms and the Life of Faith* (Minneapolis: Fortress Press, 1995), chap. 4. Burke O. Long, "Recent Field Studies in Oral Literature and the Question of Sitz im Leben," *Semeia* 5 (1976): 35–49, is especially attentive to the issues of form criticism in relation to wider issues of anthropology.

14. Ivan Engnell, "The Book of Psalms," in *Critical Essays on the Old Testament* (London: SPCK, 1970), 121, concludes: "In the Christian Church, the book of Psalms has regained something of its original *Sitz im Leben*, although the circumstances are quite different."

15. The recent argument of Albertz, *Persönliche Frömmigkeit*, in placing many of the Psalms in a domestic situation where the daily issues of life and death are alive, enhances this understanding of function.

16. The works of Ricoeur that I have found especially helpful are *Freud and Philosophy* (New Haven: Yale University Press, 1970); *Interpretation Theory* (Fort Worth: Texas Christian University Press, 1976); *The Conflict of Interpretations* (Evanston, Ill.: Northwestern University Press, 1974); and "Biblical Hermeneutics," *Semeia* 4 (1975): 29–148. I have also benefited from the essay of Loretta Dornisch, "Symbolic Systems and the Interpretation of Scripture," *Semeia* 4 (1975): 1–21. In what follows, I have tried to take account of some of the major accents of Ricoeur's programmatic work. I have sought to attend to the thrust of his argument and not merely "use" isolated points. At the same time, however, it is clear that I have not sought to fit the discussion completely into his frame of reference. It is exceedingly hazardous to offer a schema about the Psalms because it gives the appearance of imposing something on the materials. It is not my intent that the schema I offer is normative, nor that things actually moved this way in any actual, historical events. Rather, it is an attempt to exploit the heuristic value of Ricoeur's "interpretation theory" to suggest the dynamic interrelatedness of various psalms and actual human experience. It is clear that form criticism by itself cannot deal with such interrelatedness. Moreover, I find the proposals of Mowinckel and Johnson highly speculative. This attempt seeks to work from what I think is unarguable human experience without appeal to such specific, speculative notions. Thus I have no wish to suggest anything "cyclical," but rather to correlate the Psalms to the dynamic of human life, which happens in no schematic way.

17. See Ricoeur, "Biblical Hermeneutics," 114–24. This dialectic has been popularly and clearly expressed by Paul Tournier, *A Place for You* (London: SCM, 1968); see esp. 97–111 on "two movements."

18. On the failure of language and the formation of new language, I have been helped by John Dominic Crossan, whose work is summarized in *The Dark Interval* (Niles, Ill.: Argus, 1975). See also Robert Funk, *Language, Hermeneutic and the Word of God* (New York: Harper and Row, 1966). The linkage of the disorientation of life and the loss of language is nowhere more clearly expressed than in Isa 6:5. Isaiah responds to the overpowering sense of the holy by utter silence. While Isa 6:5 is conventionally translated, "I am undone," Otto Kaiser, *Isaiah 1–12* (London: SCM, 1972), 72, renders it, "I must be silent." In his commentary (80), Kaiser writes, "The presence of the Holy One 'silences' and destroys him."

Thus the linkage of being silenced and being destroyed. See Ernst Jenni, "Jesajas Berufung in der neueren Forschung," *TZ* 15 (1959): 322, on the close connection of the verbs *dāmâ* and *dāmam*, thus linkage of be silent/ be lost. The argument of Jenni is not exclusively philological, as he pays attention to the forces of the text. Jenni notes that Hab 1:3 has *dāmâ*, but the Habakkuk commentary has *hāraš*, "silence." On the verse, see the comments of Edward J. Young, *The Book of Isaiah I* (Grand Rapids: Eerdmans, 1972), 247–48, indicating the uncertainty of the versions of this point.

19. The new metaphors, says Ricoeur, *Conflict*, 369–70, "grasp more closely than any juridical figure, the relation of concrete fidelity, the bond of creation, the fact of love—in short, the dimension of gift, which no code can succeed in capturing or institutionalizing."

20. We can undoubtedly be helped by an understanding of "rites of passage," on which see Arnold von Gennep, *Rites of Passage* (Chicago: University of Chicago Press, 1960), and, derivatively, Gail Sheehy, *Passages* (New York: Dutton, 1976), and the developmental approaches of Erik Erikson, Jean Piaget, and Lawrence Kohlberg. However, it should not be missed that there is important tension between such an organismic approach to human personality, which finds developmental resources in the organism, and a view more centrally biblical, which affirms newness and gifts given from outside the organism. What is at issue is the matter of "the other" (= God) as agent.

21. Robert Gordis, "The Social Background of Wisdom Literature," in *Poets, Prophets and Sages* (Bloomington: Indiana University Press, 1971), 160–97; Brian W. Kovacs, "Is There a Class-Ethic in Proverbs?" in *Essays in Old Testament Ethics* (ed. James L. Crenshaw and John Willis; New York: KTAV, 1974), 171–89. On the problem of class-ethic, see Crenshaw, *Studies in Ancient Israelite Wisdom* (New York: KTAV, 1976), 20–22, as well as his comments on creation, wisdom, and order (26–35).

22. Claus Westermann has especially grasped the important distinction between blessing and deliverance as modes of Israel's faith, though he has not pursued the sociological dimensions of that distinction. See *Blessing in the Bible and the Life of the Church* (Philadelphia: Fortress Press, 1978), 1–14; *Elements of Old Testament Theology* (Atlanta: John Knox, 1978), pts. 2–3; and *What Does the Old Testament Say about God?* (Atlanta: John Knox Press, 1979), chs. 2–3. The books are closely paralleled but not identical. On the sociology of a religion of blessing, see Albertz, *Persönliche Frömmigkeit*.

23. Westermann, *Praise of God*, 22–30.

24. Westermann's comment, ibid., 32–33n20, is telling: he says the hymns of the Enlightenment are almost entirely descriptive; by contrast, those of Luther are for the most part declarative. This is exactly what we should expect.

25. In addition to his basic study, see Westermann, "The Role of the Lament in the Theology of the Old Testament," *Int* 28 (1974): 20–38, reprinted in his *Praise and Lament in the Psalms*; see also Brueggemann, *Psalms and the Life of Faith*, chs. 2–3.

26. Westermann, "Role of the Lament," stresses that the lament is a protest and is to be contrasted with the submission and resignation of much Christian piety under the influence of Stoicism. See also Gerstenberger, "Der klagende Mensch."

27. Still the most attractive hypothesis for understanding the break is that of Joachim Begrich ("Das priesterliche Heilsorakel," *ZAW* 52 [1934]: 81–92, reprinted in Begrich, *Gesammelte Studien zum Alten Testament* [Tbü 21; Munich: Christian Kaiser Verlag, 1964], 217–31), but it has not gone unchallenged. See especially the comments of Thomas Raitt, *A Theology of Exile* (Philadelphia: Fortress Press, 1977), 151–73.

28. Following Westermann, I have argued in *The Psalms and the Life of Faith*, ch. 4, that in the process of the psalm, something is indeed done that moves the speaker to a genuinely new situation. Gerstenberger on the same psalms can speak of "rehabilitation."

29. Ricoeur, *Freud and Philosophy*, 497. In *Conflict*, Ricoeur prefers the language of "arche and telos," "archeology and teleology."

30. David J. A. Clines, *I, He, We, and They* (JSOTSup 1; Sheffield: Sheffield University Press, 1976). On the recognition that texts bear a variety of meanings (though not unlimited), see Ricoeur, *Conflict*, 63–73. For him, both points are important, that meanings are *multiple* and *not unlimited*.

31. On the distinction made between the two, see Gerstenberger, "Jeremiah's Complaints," *JBL* 82 (1963): 405n50. In characterizing the move from law to grace, Ricoeur, *Conflict*, 339, uses language that is helpful: he speaks of the necessity of renunciation, which is "no small thing, for we prefer moral condemnation to the anguish of an existence that is both unprotected and unconsoled. All of these traits—and especially the last one—make the demystification of accusation resemble a work of *mourning*." The juxtaposition of accusation/mourning in a context of renunciation is telling in light of Psalms scholarship that relates lament to complaint. This suggests Psalm 88 may be a step past most lament psalms on the way to hope.

32. Ricoeur, *Conflict*, 96, ends his chapter with this terse and enigmatic statement: "You have fathomed that the greatest opening-out belongs to language in celebration." While one wishes he had been less cryptic, the point is helpful for our discussion.

33. On the summary and evaluation of these various hypotheses, see the discussions cited above by Johnson, Clements, and Gerstenberger.

34. Gerstenberger, "The Psalms," 199, writes, "Most form critics so far have been overly fascinated by the communal or national aspects of Israel's faith. . . . A better starting point is individual prayers and their settings." It would appear that Psalms scholarship is now tending to move toward a recovery of personal piety in the Psalms, a matter largely screened out by the dominant hypothesis of Mowinckel. In addition to the two studies of Gerstenberger, "Der klagende Mensch," and *Der bittende Mensch*, see Albertz, *Persönliche Frömmigkeit*; M. Rose, "Schultheologie und Volks-frömmigkeit," *Wort und Dienst* 13 (1975): 85–104; and, more fully, idem, *Der Ausschliesslichkeitsanspruch Jahwes* (BWANT 6; Stuttgart: W. Kohlhammer, 1975). Unfortunately, the "Volksfrömmigkeit" is in the subtitle and therefore not visible in the title as a theme of the book.

35. Westermann, *Praise of God*, 24.

36. Thus Ricoeur, *Conflict*, esp. 117, 174–76, 189, 323–30.

37. Don Ihde, "Editor's Introduction," in Ricoeur, *Conflict*, xvi, sets Hegel alongside Freud as the progenitors of the posture of suspicion. While Ricoeur recognizes Hegel and Freud as the primal articulators (323–25), it is likely that Marx and Nietzsche are more directly engaged in the issue (99, 148). See Juan Luis Segundo, *Our Idea of God* (Maryknoll, N.Y.: Orbis, 1970), 86, on the hermeneutic of suspicion more directly applied to practice. See also Dornisch, "Symbolic Systems," 6.

38. See Ricoeur, *Conflict*, 144. It is, of course, not only language that is unmasked. For all three—Freud, Marx, and Nietzsche—the major concern is a false consciousness.

39. Ricoeur, *Interpretation Theory*, 40.

40. On the *sensus plenior*, see especially Raymond E. Brown, *The Sensus Plenior of Sacred Scripture* (Baltimore: St. Mary's University, 1955), and his summary in the *Jerome Biblical Commentary* (ed. Raymond E. Brown, Joseph A. Fitzmyer, and Roland Murphy; London: Geoffrey Chapman, 1968), 615–16. As regards the New Hermeneutic, the most visible (though not clearest) presentation in English is James M. Robinson and John B. Cobb, eds., *The New Hermeneutic* (New York: Harper and Row, 1964). The work of Amos Wilder in *Theopoetic* (Philadelphia: Fortress Press, 1976) and *Early Christian Rhetoric: The Language of the*

Gospel (Cambridge, Mass.: Harvard University Press, 1971), in a more representative American way and without the heavy German casting, can be reckoned as part of the same movement, as is the programmatic intent of the journal *Semeia*. See especially Wilder's "The Word as Address and the Word as Meaning," in *The New Hermeneutic* (ed. James M. Robinson and John B. Cobb; New York: Harper and Row, 1964), 198–218. The philosophical basis of the movement has been well summarized by Richard E. Palmer, *Hermeneutics* (Evanston, Ill.: Northwestern University Press, 1969). See the useful orienting statement of Anthony C. Thiselton, "The New Hermeneutic," in *New Testament Interpretation* (ed. I. Howard Marshall; Exeter, U.K.: Paternoster, 1977), 308–33. For an appreciative but sharp criticism of structuralism, see Ricoeur, *Conflict*, 27–61, 246–66. Ricoeur discerns that its danger is that it reduces reality and language to a "closed system of signs" because there is only speech and no speaker. Ricoeur's own inclination toward hope is set against the ideology borne by structuralism. See also the strictures of Wilder, *Theopoetic*, 17–19, in which he observes that what "too often is missing is rather . . . rootedness, creaturehood, embodied humanness."

41. Thus Ricoeur, "Biblical Hermeneutics," 107, and idem, *Conflict*, 48, 288.

42. Dornisch, "Symbolic Systems," 7: "Traditional biblical hermeneutics would belong more to this second type while some aspects of biblical historical criticism would be hermeneutics of suspicion, the first type." On the penchant among scholars for "the original," see the shrewd statement of Brevard S. Childs, "The Sensus Literalis of Scripture: An Ancient and Modern Problem," in *Beiträge zur Alttestamentlichen Theologie* (ed. Herbert Donner, Robert Hanhart, and Rudolf Smend; Göttingen: Vandenhoeck and Ruprecht, 1977), 80–93. Childs's book *Introduction to the Old Testament as Scripture* (Philadelphia: Fortress Press, 1979) is an attempt to move beyond critical, analytical ways of understanding. While Childs argues in the same direction as structuralists in a concern to get beyond historicizing, his goal is very different from that of structuralists.

43. See the bold comment of Dennis McCarthy, "Exod. 3:14: History, Philology and Theology," *CBQ* 40 (1978): 311–22. Dornisch, "Symbolic Systems," 16, observes, "Hermeneutics of suspicion has led to a lack of faith, lack of meaning, and to a feeling of standing alone in the universe." In addition to the work of Childs, see the very different criticisms of method by Walter Wink, *The Bible in Human Transformation* (Philadelphia: Fortress Press, 1973), and Peter Stuhlmacher, *Historical Criticism and Theological Interpretation of Scripture* (Philadelphia: Fortress Press, 1977).

44. Ricoeur, *Freud and Philosophy*, 423–24.

45. Ibid., 543. On the need for iconoclasm, see Ricoeur, *Conflict*, 185.

46. See Ricoeur's use of the terms in "Biblical Hermeneutics," 127. In *Conflict*, 384, he urges the important correlation of text and existence. Ihde, "Editor's Introduction," xv, even speaks of the "text-self." On the dialectic, see Stuhlmacher, *Historical Criticism*, 83–91, on a "hermeneutic of consent."

47. Here I will be concerned with the plea-petition part of the psalm, which characteristically includes address, complaint, motivation, imprecation, and petition. It does not include vow and "assurance of being heard," which often serve to supersede "suspicion."

48. On lament as a primary element in the poem of Job, see Claus Westermann, *The Structure of the Book of Job* (Philadelphia: Westminster Press, 1981).

49. On the metaphor of "beastliness" in the poetry of Israel, James G. Williams, "Deciphering the Unspoken: The Theophany of Job," *HUCA* 49 (1978): 70–72, has seen the same factor in the poetry of Job that I suggest in the Psalms.

50. Such a function for a rhetorical question as a way of probing a newness is well presented by J. Gerald Janzen, "Metaphor and Reality in Hosea 11," *Semeia* 24 (1982): 7–44. Janzen suggests that Yahweh's rhetorical questions in Hos 11:8-9 are not mere rhetoric but new decisions being embraced. So I suggest in a parallel way for the speaker of questions in the psalms of lament.

51. On the waters as a threat to life, see Luis Alonso Schokel, "The Poetic Structure of Psalm 42–43," *JSOT* 1 (1976): 4–8, and idem, "Psalm 42–43: A Response," *JSOT* 3 (1977): 61–65. On the "depths" as the requirement of life from a Freudian perspective, see George Benson, *Then Joy Breaks Through* (New York: Seabury, 1972).

52. On the breaking of symbols and reusing them with fresh significance, see Ricoeur, *Conflict*, 458–93.

53. The exposition of Psalm 88 by Artur Weiser, *The Psalms* (Philadelphia: Westminster, 1962), 586–87, is typical of interpretation that moves too quickly to resolve this unresolved psalm in religious assurance. The psalm intends its user(s) to live with the painful lack of resolution.

54. Ricoeur, *Freud and Philosophy*, 460.

55. Gunkel has posited that the end-time is like the primordial time. As Mircea Eliade, in *The Myth of the Eternal Return* (London: Routledge and Kegan Paul, 1955), has shown, conventional religious myth seeks a return to the primordial timelessness as the fulfillment of the end-time.

As Ricoeur, *Conflict*, 291, has seen clearly, however, unlike conventional religious myth, there is a break in Israel between primordial time and end-time so that the hope of Israel concerns not a return but a genuine newness. Concerning the Psalms, my argument is that it is precisely the lament that causes and permits the break, so that the anticipatory hymn is genuinely a new song.

For that reason, the shattering of the lament must be honored and not quickly resolved by religious or psychological assurances for continuity. The discontinuity is genuine. (On the matter of mythic structure and "antistructure" newness, see John J. Collins, "The 'Historical Character' of the Old Testament in Recent Biblical Theology," *CBQ* 41 [1979]: 185–204.)

56. Abraham Heschel, *Who Is Man?* (Stanford, Calif.: Stanford University Press, 1966), 114–19, has understood most clearly that doxology is definitional for humanness. See also Hans Walter Wolff, *Anthropology of the Old Testament* (Philadelphia: Fortress Press, 1974), 228–29, on praise as a primary human characteristic.

57. See A. C. Thiselton, "The Parables as Language-Event," *SJT* 23 (1970): 444–45, following Heidegger.

58. See Dornisch, "Symbolic Systems," 16. In parallel fashion, Ricoeur, *Conflict*, 144, is clear about the limits of psychoanalysis. In its "pure" form, it is unwilling to make a constructive statement. That is why Ricoeur insists it must be accompanied but not displaced by a more constructive hermeneutic.

59. While taking seriously both the analytic and synchronic traditions, Ricoeur has worked toward a position of hope that is important for the Psalms. Thus in *Conflict*, 289, 395, he has been attentive to the language of confession, commitment, consent, and avowal, which reflects a radically reoriented life when it "renounces self-determination." He has given major attention to this in *Freedom and Nature* (Evanston, Ill.: Northwestern University Press, 1966): "To consent does not in the least mean to give up, if, in spite of appearances, the world is a possible stage for freedom. When I say, this is my place, I adopt it, I do not yield, I acquiesce. That is really so; for 'all things work for the good for those who love God, who are called according to his plan.' Thus consent would have its 'poetic' root in hope, as decision in love and effort in the gift of power" (467). "The way of consent leads through hope which awaits *something else*. Hope says: The world is not the final home of freedom" (480).

60. Ricoeur, *Freud and Philosophy*, 494.

61. Ibid., 460; idem, *Conflict*, 330.

62. Ricoeur, *Freud and Philosophy*, 496; see Dornisch, "Symbolic Systems," 7.

63. This is evident in all Ricoeur's work, but most direcdy in *Interpretation Theory* and his Sprunt Lectures of 1978.

64. Thiselton, "New Hermeneutic," provides a full bibliography.

65. Hans-Georg Gadamer, *Truth and Method* (New York: Seabury, 1975). Palmer, *Hermeneutics*, 162ff., has usefully placed Gadamer in historical perspective.

66. Robert W. Funk, "Structure in the Narrative Parables of Jesus," *Semeia* 2 (1974): 51–73; and idem, "The Good Samaritan as Metaphor," ibid., 74–81. In these articles, Funk has moved from explicitly hermeneutical to structuralist questions, but the two cannot be separated. See John Dominic Crossan, *In Parables: The Challenge of the Historical Jesus* (New York: Harper and Row, 1973). A number of his papers are presented in *Semeia* 1 and 2. His more theoretical work on language is in *The Dark Interval* and *Raid on the Articulate* (New York: Harper and Row, 1976).

67. In utilizing Ricoeur's theory of language, and to relate the Psalms to that tradition of scholarship, we must not proceed without a critical awareness. The discussion of language and hermeneutics has proceeded too much on purely formal grounds as though language per se had evocative qualities. That may be so, but it is not the assumption made here. That is, our formal understandings of language must be informed by the substantive claims made by the content, use, and function of quite *concrete* language. That is, I am helped by Ricoeur's suggestions, but my argument is not about language in general but about the Psalms of Israel in the faith and life of Israel. What gives this language its evocative power for Israel are the memories of Israel; the hopes of Israel; and the discernment of the gifts, actions, blessings, and judgments of God at work in their common life. Speech has this power because it correlates with the realities in which Israel trusted. The language itself is not the reality but is the trusted mode of disclosure of that reality.

68. Unfortunately, we do not have a careful theological criticism of Heidegger's program as it has decisively affected theological interpretation, though Thiselton has made a beginning in this direction. It is unfortunate that the "new literary critics" seem inattentive to the ideological dangers in the categories of Heidegger, which are not disposed toward the promissory, which is so crucial for biblical faith. Ricoeur, in *Conflict*, seems prepared to move beyond these categories, precisely in a promissory direction.

69. Ricoeur, "Biblical Hermeneutics," 108–25. He follows the work of William Beardslee, Norman Perrin, Robert Funk, and Dominic Crossan cited there.

70. A. C. Thiselton, "The Supposed Power of Words in the Biblical Writings," *JTS* 25 (1974): 283–99, has offered a quite suggestive way of thinking about the "power of the word" that avoids the unguarded formal claims that have now been refuted by James Barr. Thiselton is clear that the function of language depends on which language is used and in what context. That is, there is no absolute or universal language. But there are concrete languages enmeshed in and related to concrete communities of historical experience. The language of the Psalms may be closely paralleled in other communities, e.g., Babylonian, but the Psalms function and claim differently because of Israel's experience with this shape of reality.

71. On muteness in relation to powerlessness, see Dorothee Sölle, *Suffering* (Philadelphia: Fortress Press, 1975), 68–86, and Walter Brueggemann, *The Prophetic Imagination* (Philadelphia: Fortress Press, 1978), esp. ch. 3.

72. Ricoeur, *Conflict*, 291–92, is attentive to the distinctiveness of Israel on this point: "This switch of themes is the expression of an overturning of fundamental motifs. A new category of experience is born: that of 'before God,' of which the Jewish *berit*, the Covenant, is the witness." Eliade, *Myth of the Eternal Return*, 160–62, has discerned what many of his followers ignore and what Ricoeur takes most seriously, that in Israel there is a fundamental break with that common religious future that is a return to primal reality. The reality of newness in Israel is not primal but eschatological. "Basically, the horizon of archetypes and repetition cannot be transcended with impunity unless we accept a philosophy of freedom that does not exclude God. And indeed this proved to be true when the horizon of archetypes and repetition was transcended, for the first time, by Judaeo-Christianism, which introduced a new category into religious experience, the category of faith. It must not be forgotten that, if Abraham's faith can be defined as 'for God everything is possible,' the faith of Christianity implies that everything is also possible for man" (160). Eliade then quotes Mark 11:22-24. It is remarkable that Eliade, who characteristically seeks the commonalities, is attentive to this distinctiveness. In his own way, Eliade makes the same point as Ricoeur in his tilt toward hope. Against the structuralists that ignore Eliade's point, Ricoeur, *Conflict*, 48–52, suggests that the usual examples for structuralism are drawn from religions very different in mode from that of Israel. Thus he contrasts totemistic and kerygmatic modes. The same peculiarity of Israel is

acknowledged by Northrop Frye, "The Critical Path: An Essay on the Social Context of Literary Criticism," in *In Search of Literary Theory*, ed. Morton W. Bloomfield (Ithaca, N.Y.: Cornell University Press, 1972), 107–13, even though he is inclined toward Jungian categories of commonality. It is precisely in Israel that the steady practice of suspicion (on the one hand, by the laments, on the other, by the prophets) makes new, prospective symbolization possible.

73. While it is beyond the scope of this essay, we should note the judgment of Jürgen Habermas that the practice of criticism is "anticipatory rationality." See Thomas McCarthy, *The Critical Theory of Jürgen Habermas* (Cambridge, Mass.: MIT Press, 1978), 75–91. The telling subheading of McCarthy's discussion is, "The Emancipatory Interest of Critical Theory." Brevard Childs, *Introduction*, 513–18, has seen that, in canonical form, the Psalms are "highly eschatological." That is, they criticize the present in an anticipatory way.

74. Ricoeur, *Freud and Philosophy*, 175; see 521.

75. Ibid., 496.

76. Ricoeur, "Biblical Hermeneutics," 125. See idem, *Conflict*, 185–95, on the essential linkage of iconoclasm and grace.

77. Dornisch, "Symbolic Systems," 8.

78. See the discussion of Gerstenberger, Albertz, and Rose cited in n. 34. In addition, George W. Anderson has given a lecture indicating this to be the direction of his own psalms research. In such a move, care must be taken that categories are not used that encourage a kind of religious privatism, for the experience of disorientation and reorientation concerns public as well as personal issues. It is important that Westermann has included both personal (personal lament, thanksgiving song) and public (communal lament, hymn) songs in his interpretation. Mary Douglas, *Natural Symbols* (London: Barrie and Jenkins, 1973), has shown the close and reciprocal relationship of public symbols and personal involvement either in embrace or in revolt.

79. This is the "new creation" about which Mowinckel has hypothesized. Werner Meyer, *Untersuchungen zur Formensprache der babylonischen 'Gebetsbeschwörungen'* (Rome: Pontifical Biblical Institute, 1976), 331 (quoted by Delbert Hillers, "A Study of Psalm 148," *CBQ* 40 [1978]: 332), speaks of a "newly won 'wholeness.'"

80. Ricoeur, "Biblical Hermeneutics," 94.

81. See Thiselton, "New Hermeneutic," 318–23, on language and world-formation. This central insight of the New Hermeneutic needs to be brought into relation with sociological realism. As it stands, the

proponents of the New Hermeneutic seem uninterested in the actual shape of the new world. The practice of linguistic imagination, however, must be coupled with political and economic realities. Thus the new world formed by Israel's new song was one in which the agenda of justice and righteousness was uppermost (Pss 96:13; 97:2, 10-12; 98:9; 99:4). Imagination is not an end in itself but serves the new concrete human world that is promised and given by God. On the linkage of imagination and politics, see Wilder, *Theopoetic*, ch. 3, in which he likens early Christianity to "guerrilla theater."

Chapter 2: God at Work in the Word

1. One need only mention such figures as Rashi, Qimhi, Augustine, Luther, and Calvin, among many others.

2. Athanasius, "A Letter of Athanasius, Our Holy Father, Archbishop of Alexandria, to Marcellinus on the Interpretation of the Psalms," in *The Life of Antony and the Letter to Marcellinus* (trans. Robert C. Gregg; Classics of Western Spirituality; New York: Paulist, 1980), ch. 2. Athanasius demonstrates his point at length in the chapters that follow. Martin Luther, "Preface to the Psalter," in *Luther's Works* (ed. Theodore Bachmann; Philadelphia: Fortress Press, 1960), 35:253.

3. Hans-Joachim Kraus, *Theology of the Psalms* (trans. Keith Crim; Minneapolis: Augsburg, 1986), 12.

4. To some extent, the work of Erhard S. Gerstenberger runs counter to such attempts, since he sees the Psalter as containing within itself a number of different themes and images stemming from the various periods of its historical development. Cf. his "Theologies in the Book of Psalms," in *The Book of Psalms: Composition and Reception* (ed. Peter W. Flint and Patrick D. Miller; Leiden: Brill, 2005), 603–25.

5. For the movement from Torah to praise, see Walter Brueggemann, "Bounded by Obedience and Praise: The Psalms as Canon," *JSOT* 50 (1991): 63–92. In that article, Brueggemann also sees a movement from lament to praise, as does Gerald H. Wilson, "The Shape of the Book of Psalms," *Int* 46 (1992): 138–39. For the move from a concern with human kingship to divine kingship, see the many works of Wilson, beginning with his *The Editing of the Hebrew Psalter* (SBLDS 76; Chico, Calif.: Scholars, 1985).

6. See especially Jerome F. D. Creach, *The Destiny of the Righteous in the Psalms* (St. Louis: Chalice, 2008).

7. One also finds a concern for God's relationship with the natural world in the Psalms, especially in the psalms of praise.

8. Gerhard von Rad, *Old Testament Theology*, vol. 1, trans. D. M. G. Stalker (New York: Harper and Row, 1962), 356.

9. Ibid., 1:356.

10. Ibid.

11. Kraus, *Theology*, 13, citing von Rad, *Old Testament Theology*, 1:105–6.

12. Kraus, *Theology*, 13.

13. Ibid., 14, citation from Karl Barth, *Einführung in die evangelische Theologie* (Zürich: EVZ Verlag, 1962), 180–81.

14. Kraus, *Theology*, 14.

15. It is of interest that Kraus sees the "wisdom statements in the Psalms" as providing a "significant starting point for a theology of the Psalms." Ibid., 15–16. While these statements are clearly important, they are often the parts of the Psalms less likely to be in the form of a second-person direct address to God.

16. On this, see Athanasius, "Letter," ch. 11, where he notes the "astonishing" ability of the person praying to utter the psalm "as his own words." For Athanasius, it is this ability that makes the psalms distinctive even among the other books of Scripture. For a more detailed discussion of Athanasius on this issue, see my *Defining the Sacred Songs: Genre, Tradition and the Post-Critical Interpretation of the Psalms* (JSOTSup 218; Sheffield: Sheffield Academic, 1999), 108–16.

17. The relevance of Buber's model to the Psalms may be seen in Herbert J. Levine, *Sing Unto God A New Song: A Contemporary Reading of the Psalms* (Bloomington: Indiana University Press, 1995), 79–129. See also Robert Moore Jumonville and Robert Woods, "A Role-Taking Theory of Praying the Psalms: Using the Psalms as a Model for Structuring the Life of Prayer," *JBS* 3 (2003): esp. 53–56. Both of these sources also note the similar stress on dialogue and participation in the discourse theory of Mikhail Bakhtin and bring that to bear on the Psalms. Walter Brueggemann has also related Buber and the Psalms in his "The Psalms in Theological Use: On Incommensurability and Mutuality," in *The Book of Psalms: Composition and Reception* (ed. Peter W. Flint and Patrick D. Miller; Leiden: Brill, 2005), 583–84.

18. Hermann Gunkel and Joachim Begrich, *An Introduction to the Psalms: The Genres of the Religious Lyric of Israel* (trans. James D. Nogalski; Macon, Ga.: Mercer University Press, 1998), 20–21.

19. See, for example, Westermann's *Praise and Lament in the Psalms* (trans. Keith R. Crim and Richard N. Soulen; Atlanta: John Knox, 1981).

20. Kraus, *Theology*, 14.

21. See especially Mowinckel's *Psalmenstudien*, vol. 2: *Das Thronbesteigungsfest Jahwäs und der Ursprung der Eschatologie* (Amsterdam: Schippers,

1961 [1922]), 21. See also his *The Psalms in Israel's Worship* (Nashville: Abingdon, 1962) 15–22.

22. Such as his view that Israel had a new year's festival similar to that of its neighbors.

23. Mowinckel, *Psalmenstudien*, 2:21.

24. Cf. especially his *Israel's Praise: Doxology against Idolatry and Ideology* (Philadelphia: Fortress, 1988). For an analysis of the ways in which Brueggmann has appropriated Mowinckel's view of cult for his analysis of the Psalms, see my *Sacred Songs*, 86–107.

25. Athanasius, "Letter," ch. 10. On this again see my *Sacred Songs*, 108–16.

26. Athanasius, "Letter," ch. 11.

27. James L. Mays, "Means of Grace: The Benefits of Psalmic Prayer," and "With These Words: The Language World of the Psalms," both in *The Lord Reigns: A Theological Handbook to the Psalms* (Louisville: Westminster John Knox, 1994), 40–41, 3–5 respectively.

28. See my *Sacred Songs*, 116–23.

29. For examples of those who see Scripture as having sacramental power, see Sandra M. Schneiders, *The Revelatory Text: Interpreting the New Testament as Sacred Scripture* (San Francisco: HarperSanFrancisco, 1991), esp. 40–42; John Breck, *The Power of the Word in the Worshiping Church* (New York: St. Vladimir's Seminary Press, 1986), 11–22.

30. Especially important along these lines for the theology of the Psalms has been William Brown's *Seeing the Psalms: A Theology of Metaphor* (Louisville: Westminster John Knox, 2002).

31. James L. Mays, "The Center of the Psalms: 'The LORD Reigns' as Root Metaphor," in *The Lord Reigns: A Theological Handbook to the Psalms* (Louisville: Westminster John Knox, 1994), 12–22. For William Brown, God as king is "one of the most prominent metaphors in the Psalter" because of "its integrative and generative power." Brown, *Seeing the Psalms*, 188.

32. Mays, "Language World," 11.

33. See Brown, *Seeing the Psalms*, for a perceptive discussion of many of these as well as a useful discussion of the formative power of metaphor in the Psalms.

34. So Pss 6:2; 41:4; cf. 30:2.

35. So Pss 103:3; 107:20; cf. 147:3.

36. So, for example, Pss 6:2; 41:4 parallel "heal" (*rpʾ*) with "be gracious" (*ḥnn*), while Psalms 107 and 147 contain descriptions of God's power over the natural world.

37. So, for example, Ibn Ezra sees David as writing Psalm 6 prophetically about Israel's being like sick people during their time in exile. *Midrash Tehillim* also sees the physical symptoms described here as metaphors for the suffering of Israel among the nations.

38. See, for example, Rashi and David Qimhi on Ps 30:3, as well as Qimhi on Pss 41:5; 103:3. The Christian tradition is similar in this regard. For an account of the way the Psalms were seen by Augustine and the early monastics as a means of healing the emotions, see Michael C. McCarthy, SJ, "'We Are Your Books': Augustine, the Bible, and the Practice of Authority," *JAAR* 75 (2007): 340–41.

39. While the healing of sickness and the forgiveness of sin are often connected in the Psalms (as in Pss 41:5; 103:3), it is only elsewhere in the Bible (Hos 14:5; Jer 3:22) and in the later interpretive tradition that one finds references to God's "healing" sinfulness.

40. The psalm does not use the word *rp'*, and the only possible physical distress is to be fond in the reference to the bones that God has broken in v. 8.

41. See, for example, *Midrash Tehillim* and Augustine's *Enarrationes* on this psalm.

42. So, for example, Cassiodorus sees the penitential psalms as "suitable medicine prescribed for the human race," from which "we obtain most health giving baths for our souls." *Cassiodorus: Explanation of the Psalms* (trans. P. G. Walsh; Ancient Christian Writers 51; Mahwah, N.J.: Paulist, 1990), 1:98.

43. So Athanasius sees the psalms as "therapy," the means of "healing" passion through "speaking and acting." "Letter," chs. 13, 10. Augustine is similar, as noted by McCarthy, "Augustine," 340–41.

44. The concept of teaching is covered by a number of different Hebrew roots, including *yrh*, *lmd*, and *yd'*.

45. James L. Mays, "The Place of the Torah Psalms in the Psalter," in *The Lord Reigns: A Theological Handbook to the Psalms* (Louisville: Westminster John Knox, 1994), 131–32. According to Mays, "The Psalms are the liturgy for those whose concern and delight is the torah of the LORD." On God as teacher, see Brown, *Seeing the Psalms*, 193–95. Brown notes that "this metaphor enhances God's authoritative claim on the psalmist and the community. Though not as vividly prevalent as the royal or warrior imagery among the psalms, the teacher metaphor is fundamental to the final coherence of the Psalter as a source of instruction, indeed, as the *tora* of YHWH (Ps 1:2-3)."

46. It is important to note that what is taught includes but is not restricted to specific statutes and commandments. One also seeks to be

taught God's "way(s)," a term that includes the type of behavior both exhibited and required by God. In such a way, the individual not only learns about his or her own responsibilities to God; he or she also learns about God, God's ways in the world, and God's way of being in relationship with him- or herself.

47. See *Midrash Tehillim* on Pss 22:8; 57:4. According to the comments on 22:8, "Because of David all the children of Israel sat down and occupied themselves with Torah" (translation from William G. Braude, *The Midrash on Psalms* (New Haven: Yale University Press, 1959), 1:305. According to an accompanying midrash, David's harp awakened David by playing on its own. For other places in which David was seen to be a student of Torah, see *Midrash Tehillim* on 25:4; 119:28.

48. That these interpreters see this teaching as including what is found in the book of Psalms may be seen from the parallel they saw between Moses and the five books of the Torah and David and the five books of the Psalms. So *Midrash Tehillim* on Ps 1:2: "As Moses gave five books of laws to Israel, so David gave five books of Psalms to Israel" (trans. Braude, *Midrash*, 5).

49. This formulation is from Calvin's preface to Louis Budé's French translation of the Psalms, as found in Rudolphe Peter, "Calvin et la traduction des Psaumes de Louis Budé," *Revue d'histoire et de philosophie religieuses* 42 (1962): 188, and quoted by Hermann J. Selderhuis, *Calvin's Theology of the Psalms* (Grand Rapids: Baker Academic, 2007), 24. Selderhuis notes that in the preface to his own commentary on the Psalms, "Calvin's emphasis on the teaching aspect of the Psalms is rather conspicuous." In this preface, Calvin lists a number of things that the Psalms teach, including how to pray and the way of the cross.

50. So, for example, in his comments on Ps 25:4, Calvin notes David's need for divine instruction, despite his being a prophet with so much wisdom, and then compares that with our own greater need for God to illuminate us. For the importance to Calvin of David's role as a model, see Barbara Pitkin, "Imitation of David: David as Paradigm for Faith in Calvin's Exegesis of Psalms," *Sixteenth Century Journal* 24 (1993): 843–63.

51. John Calvin, *Commentary on the Book of Psalms* (trans. James Anderson; Grand Rapids: Baker, 1989), 1:xxxvii.

52. Von Rad, *Old Testament Theology*, 2:377.

53. Ibid., 2:377.

54. Ibid., 1:401, 403. For von Rad, "The words of prayer about the abandonment of the righteous only reached fulfillment in the sufferings of Christ." Ibid., 2:377.

55. Samuel Terrien, *The Elusive Presence: The Heart of Biblical Theology* (San Francisco: Harper & Row, 1978), 311. For Terrien, the poets who composed the individual laments showed a depth of theological perceptiveness that points to the authenticity of their encounter with the divine (307).

56. Ibid., 326.

57. See especially Creach, *Destiny of the Righteous*.

58. For Creach, "being in the presence of God is the destiny of the righteous." Ibid., 18.

59. Ibid., 87. Creach sees these as the "embodied hope" of the righteous.

60. Claus Westermann, "The Role of the Lament in the Theology of the Old Testament," in *Praise and Lament in the Psalms* (trans. Keith R. Crim and Richard N. Soulen; Atlanta: John Knox, 1981), 264.

61. Ibid., 272–73.

62. Walter Brueggemann, *The Message of the Psalms: A Theological Commentary* (Minneapolis: Augsburg, 1984), 173.

63. Ibid., 176.

64. Claus Westermann, "The Structure and History of the Lament in the Old Testament," and "Role of the Lament," in *Praise and Lament in the Psalms* (trans. Keith R. Crim and Richard N. Soulen; Atlanta: John Knox, 1981), 206–13, 265, 274–75. Westermann wonders whether this is the result of exposure to Greek thought, though he also sees it as a result of a Pauline emphasis on human sinfulness rather than human suffering.

65. Westermann, "Role of the Lament," 274–75.

66. Walter Brueggemann, "The Costly Loss of Lament," in *The Psalms and the Life of Faith*, ed. Patrick D. Miller (Minneapolis: Fortress Press, 1995), 98–111.

67. For the view that the "mutuality" evident in the lament psalms challenges God's "incommensurability" in a way that makes God vulnerable, see Brueggemann, "The Psalms in Theological Use," 581–602.

68. James Luther Mays, "Means of Grace: The Benefits of Psalmic Prayer," in *The Lord Reigns: A Theological Handbook to the Psalms* (Louisville: Westminster John Knox, 1994), 40. See also Howard Neil Wallace, *Words to God, Word from God: The Psalms in the Prayer and Preaching of the Church* (Burlington: Ashgate, 2005), 15: "We witness divine grace in God's gift of words through which we might in turn speak back to God."

69. So, for example, Gregory of Nyssa, *Commentary on the Inscriptions of the Psalms* (trans. Casimir McCambly, OCSO; Brookline, Mass.; Hellenic College, n.d.), 2:11; Athanasius, "Letter," ch. 31, 33. For more general comments on the role of the Holy Spirit in prayer and liturgy,

see Karl Rahner, SJ, *On Prayer* (New York: Paulist, 1958), 20–30; Breck, *Power of the Word*, 46; Karl Barth, *Evangelical Theology: An Introduction* (trans. Grover Foley; New York: Holt, Rinehart and Winston, 1963), 169–70.

70. Gregory, *Commentary*, 2:11. In conjunction with this image, Gregory sees the Spirit as the teacher who teaches how to conform our souls through virtue to God.

71. On the early Christian view of Jesus as the one who prays the Psalms both with regard to himself and with regard to his body, the church, see O. Linton, "Interpretation of the Psalms in the Early Church," *Studia Patristica* 4, TU 79 (1961): 143–56. See also the similar modern treatment of Dietrich Bonhoeffer, *Psalms: The Prayer Book of the Bible* (trans. James H. Burtness; Minneapolis: Augsburg, 1970), 50–55, and my discussion in *Sacred Songs*, 154–60.

72. See, for example, *Shir. R.* 4.3, where David is seen as the one who makes all the songs of Israel pleasing to God.

73. So Peter E. Fink, SJ, has noted that liturgy is "first and foremost the *work of God in the people* transforming them, us, and all human life into God's own glory" (emphasis original). "Liturgy and Spirituality: A Timely Intersection," in *Liturgy and Spirituality in Context: Perspectives on Prayer and Culture* (ed. Eleanor Bernstein, CSJ; Collegeville, Minn.: Liturgical, 1990), 61. On this, see also my "The Sacramental Function of the Psalms in Contemporary Scholarship and Liturgical Practice," in *Psalms and Practice: Worship, Virtue, and Authority* (ed. Stephen Breck Reid; Collegeville, Minn.: Liturgical, 2001), 78–89.

74. Among many examples of interpreters who see David as the model of repentance to others, see Martin Luther, *Selected Psalms* 1:318–319, and *Midrash Tehillim* on Ps 51:6.

75. So Brevard S. Childs, *Introduction to the Old Testament as Scripture* (Philadelphia: Fortress, 1979), 517–18: "However one explains it, the final form of the Psalter is highly eschatological in nature. It looks toward the future and passionately yearns for its arrival. Even when the psalmist turns briefly to reflect on the past in praise of the 'great things which Yahweh has done,' invariably the movement shifts and again the hope of salvation is projected into the future (Ps. 126.6). The perspective of Israel's worship in the Psalter is eschatologically oriented." Mays also has noted how the hope for the coming kingdom of God functions as the eschatological context of torah-piety in the Psalms. "Torah Psalms," 134.

Chapter 3: The Destiny of the Righteous and the Theology of the Psalms

1. The classic expression of this understanding of the Psalms as "Israel's answer" (*Antwort*) is expressed by Gerhard von Rad, *Old Testament Theology*, vol. 1: *The Theology of Israel's Historical Traditions* (trans. D. M. G. Stalker; New York: Harper & Row, 1962), 355–70; it is the starting point for the treatment of the subject by Hans-Joachim Kraus, *Theology of the Psalms* (trans. Keith Crim; Minneapolis: Augsburg, 1986); and H. Spieckermann, *Heilsgegenwart: Eine Theologie der Psalmen* (Göttingen: Vandenhoeck and Ruprecht, 1989), see 7–20; more recently the notion of the Psalms as *Antwort* has been used by Hans-Peter Mathys to argue for the theological and summative use of late psalms in the Psalter and of psalm-like material elsewhere in the Old Testament; see *Dichter und Beter: Theologen aus spätalttestamentlicher Zeit* (OBO 32; Göttingen: Vandenhoeck and Ruprecht, 1994).

2. James Luther Mays, *The Lord Reigns: A Theological Handbook to the Psalms* (Louisville: Westminster John Knox, 1994), 12, describes the task as "the attempt to discern and describe a theological dimension assumed by and/or expressed in the Psalms in all their variety."

3. For a full discussion of this proposal see Jerome F. D. Creach, *The Destiny of the Righteous in the Psalms* (St. Louis: Chalice, 2008); see the similar argument by Christoph Levin, "Das Gebetbuch der Gerechten. Literargeschichtliche Beobachtungen am Psalter," *ZTK* 90 (1993): 355–81.

4. Von Rad, *Old Testament Theology*, 1:370.

5. For more on the kingship of God as organizing center, see Mays, *The Lord Reigns*, 12–22; J. Clinton McCann Jr. offers a helpful essay with similar trajectory; see "Righteousness, Justice, and Peace: A Contemporary Theology of the Psalms," *HBT* 23, no. 2 (2001): 111–31.

6. Citations of psalms refer to verses in Hebrew; when English verses differ they appear in parentheses.

7. Mays, *The Lord Reigns*, 27.

8. As Patrick D. Miller notes concerning the righteous and the wicked, "How these two groups act, the way they go—whether one means their path of life or their ultimate fate—is very much the subject matter of the psalms;" see "The Beginning of the Psalter," in *The Shape and Shaping of the Psalter* (ed. J. Clinton McCann Jr.; JSOTSup 159; Sheffield: JSOT Press, 1993), 85.

9. See especially the seminal work of Gerald H. Wilson, *The Editing of the Hebrew Psalter* (SBLDS 76; Chico, Calif.: Scholars Press, 1985); see also Nancy deClaissé-Walford, *An Introduction to the Psalms: A Song from Ancient Israel* (St. Louis: Chalice, 2004); the essays in J. Clinton McCann Jr., ed., *The Shape and Shaping of the Psalter*; James L. Mays, "The Place of the Torah-Psalms in the Psalter," *JBL* (1987), 1–12; reprinted in *The Lord Reigns*, 128–35; this recent work is summarized by David Howard, "The Psalms in Current Study," in *Interpreting the Psalms: Issues and Approaches* (ed. Philip S. Johnston and David G. Firth; Leicester, U.K.: Apollos, 2005), 23–40; and by Patrick D. Miller Jr., "The Psalter as a Book of Theology," in *Psalms in Community: Jewish and Christian Textual, Liturgical, and Artistic Traditions* (ed. Harold W. Attridge and Margot E. Fassler; SBLSymS 25; Atlanta: SBL Press, 2003), 87–98.

10. See the discussion in Jerome F. D. Creach, *Yahweh as Refuge and the Editing of the Hebrew Psalter* (JSOTSup 217; Sheffield: Sheffield Academic, 1996), 77–79.

11. On the significant role of this term in the Psalter see J. Clinton McCann Jr., "Psalms," in *The New Interpreter's Bible* (Nashville: Abingdon, 1996), 4:666–67; idem, "The Shape of Book One of the Psalter and the Shape of Human Happiness," in *The Book of Psalms: Composition and Reception* (ed. Peter W. Flint and Patrick D. Miller Jr.; VTSup; Leiden: Brill, 2005), 340–48.

12. See Creach, *Yahweh as Refuge*, 74–77.

13. Miller, "The Beginning of the Psalter," 85.

14. Ibid., 88–89.

15. This dual identity of the righteous is quite apparent in the many psalms that are spoken by an individual but include invitations for the people; Pss 129, 130, and 131 are parade examples; see Joachim Becker, *Israel deutet seine Psalmen: Urform und Neuinterpretation in den Psalmen* (Stuttgart: Verlag Katholisches Bibelwerk, 1967), 22–24, and esp. 41–68.

16. Mays, *The Lord Reigns*, 123.

17. Ibid.

18. Gerald H. Wilson argues that psalms at the breaks between collections often show signs of editorial intentionality; see "The Use of Royal Psalms at the 'Seams' of the Hebrew Psalter," *JSOT* 35 (1986): 85–94.

19. See again the insightful essay by McCann, "The Shape of Book I of the Psalter," 340–48.

20. For a radically different interpretation of the psalm and its setting, see Gerstenberger, *Psalms: Part I* (FOTL 14; Grand Rapids: Eerdmans), 174–77.

21. Frank-Lothar Hossfeld and Erich Zenger, *Psalms 2: A Commentary on Psalms 51–100* (trans. Linda M. Maloney; Hermeneia; Minneapolis: Fortress Press, 2005), 216.

22. The book is like the "book of remembrance" in Mal 3:16-18: "And a book of remembrance was written before him of those who revered the Lord and thought on his name. 'They shall be mine,' says the Lord of hosts, 'my special possession'" (see also Exod 32:32-33; Phil 4:3; Rev 3:5).

23. G. Braulik, *Psalm 40 und der Gottesknecht* (Würzburg: Echter, 1975), 197–201.

24. Note that the question of God's *ḥesed* ("steadfast love") to his anointed was raised in Psalm 89:50 (49) and addressed in Psalms 90:14; 92:3 (2); 103:4, 17; 106:1, 45.

25. In *The Lord Reigns*, 12–22.

26. See the concern for the future of the righteous, for example, in Pss 92:9, 14-15; 101:8; 103:6.

27. This thesis concerning the purpose of Pss 90–106 is now widely accepted; it is expressed by Wilson, *Editing*, 214–28.

28. See Creach, *The Destiny of the Righteous in the Psalms*, 86–149; for the conception of king, Zion, and Torah as the "embodied hope" of the righteous, I am indebted to Walter Brueggemann's characterization of Israel's "embodied testimony" in *Theology of the Old Testament: Testimony, Dispute, Advocacy* (Minneapolis: Fortress Press, 1997), 567–704.

29. On the significance of this line, see Jerome F. D. Creach, "Like a Tree Planted by the Temple Stream: The Portrait of the Righteous in Psalm 1:3," *CBQ* 61, no. 1 (1999): 34–46.

30. On this point, see the insightful argument of David P. Moessner, "*Two* Lords 'at the Right Hand'? The Psalms and an Intertextual Reading of Peter's Pentecost Speech (Acts 2:14-36)," in *Literary Studies in Luke-Acts: Essays in Honor of Joseph B. Tyson* (ed. Richard P. Thompson and Thomas E. Phillips; Macon, Ga.: Mercer University Press, 1998), 215–32.

31. The expression "abiding theological witness" and its implication for understanding the Psalms as scripture is borrowed from Christopher R. Seitz, *Word without End: The Old Testament as Abiding Theological Witness* (Grand Rapids: Eerdmans, 1998), esp. 3–12, 61–74.

Chapter 4: The Single Most Important Text in the Entire Bible

1. John Dominic Crossan, *The Birth of Christianity: Discovering What Happened in the Years Immediately after the Execution of Jesus* (San Francisco: HarperSanFrancisco, 1998), 575.

2. Frank-Lothar Hossfeld and Erich Zenger, *Psalms 2: A Commentary on Psalms 51-100* (trans. Linda M. Maloney; Hermeneia; Minneapolis: Fortress Press, 2005), 337.

3. Crossan, *Birth of Christianity*, 575–76.

4. Hossfeld and Zenger, *Psalms 2*, 333.

5. Ibid.

6. Lowell K. Handy, "Sounds, Words, and Meanings in Psalm 82," *JSOT* 47 (1990): 62–63.

7. Hossfeld and Zenger, *Psalms 2*, 336.

8. Konrad Schaefer, *Psalms* (Berit Olam: Studies in Hebrew Narrative and Poetry; Collegeville, Minn.: Liturgical, 2001), 203.

9. Gerald H. Wilson, "The Use of Royal Psalms at the 'Seams' of the Psalter," *JSOT* 35 (1986): 92; see also idem, *The Editing of the Hebrew Psalter* (SBLDS 76; Chico, Calif.: Scholars, 1985), 209–14.

10. Paul Westermeyer, *Let Justice Sing: Hymnody and Justice* (American Essays in Liturgy; Collegeville, Minn.: Liturgical, 1998), 29–31.

11. For discussions of the theological significance of the prayers for help, including the importance of *hesed* in the Psalms, see also J. Clinton McCann Jr., "Righteousness, Justice, and Peace: A Contemporary Theology of the Psalms," *Horizons in Biblical Theology* 23, no. 2 (December 2001): 119–23; and idem, "The Book of Psalms: Introduction, Commentary, and Reflections," in *The New Interpreter's Bible* (Nashville: Abingdon, 1996), 4:668–72.

12. William H. Bellinger Jr., "The Psalms as a Place to Begin for Old Testament Theology," in *Psalms and Practice: Worship, Virtue, and Authority* (ed. Stephen Breck Reid; Collegeville, Minn.: Liturgical, 2001), 36.

13. John Goldingay, *Psalms*, vol. 2: *Psalms 42–89* (Baker Commentary on the Old Testament Wisdom and Psalms; Grand Rapids: Baker Academic, 2007), 570 (emphasis added).

Chapter 5: The Theology of the Imprecatory Psalms

1. See Erich Zenger, *A God of Vengeance? Understanding the Psalms of Divine Wrath* (trans. Linda M. Maloney; Louisville: Westminster John Knox, 1996). He states that Pss 12, 58, 83, 109, and 137 are imprecatory. I add Psalms 94 and 129 to Zenge's list. All quotations from Scripture, unless otherwise noted, are from the NRSV.

2. See also Pss 7, 52, 55, 79, 97, and 140. John N. Day, in "The Imprecatory Psalms and Christian Ethics," *Bibliotheca Sacra* 159 (2002): 169,

maintains that over one hundred verses in the book of Psalms contain imprecatory words.

3. J. Carl Laney, "A Fresh Look at the Imprecatory Psalms," *Bibliotheca Sacra* 1 (1981): 35.

4. Artur Weiser, *The Psalms: A Commentary* (trans. Herbert Hartwell; Philadelphia: Westminster, 1962), 432.

5. Hans-Joachim Kraus, *Psalms 60–150* (trans. Hilton C. Oswald; Minneapolis: Fortress Press, 1993), 504.

6. Edwin McNeill Poteat, "Exposition on Psalms 42–89," in *The Interpreter's Bible* (ed. George Arthur Buttrick; Nashville: Abingdon, 1955), 4:450–51.

7. "Canon" is, of course, a word first applied to Scripture by the Christian Council of Carthage in 397. When speaking of the Hebrew Bible corpus of literature, it is better to use the term "authoritative literature."

8. All of the imprecatory psalms are attested except Psalm 58. Psalm 12 is included in 11QPs[c] and 5/6 HevPs; Psalm 83 in MasPs[a]; Psalm 94 in 4QPs[b] and 1PPs[a]; Psalm 109 in 4QPs[e], 4QPs[f], and 11QPs[a]; Psalm 129 in 11QPs[a] and 4QPs[e]; and Psalm 137 in 11QPs[a]. See James Vanderkam and Peter Flint, *The Meaning of the Dead Sea Scrolls* (San Francisco: HarperSanFrancisco, 2002), 419–22.

9. James A. Sanders, "Canonical Context and Canonical Criticism," in *From Sacred Story to Sacred Text* (Philadelphia: Fortress Press, 1987), 166.

10. James A. Sanders, *Torah and Canon* (Philadelphia: Fortress Press, 1972), xv.

11. Picking and choosing which biblical texts one will read and appropriate into one's life of faith and which texts one will choose not to read and appropriate is creating, in effect, "a canon within a canon," a common phenomenon in faith communities. For an excellent discussion of the concept of canon, see Lee Martin McDonald and James A. Sanders, eds., *The Canon Debate* (Peabody, Mass.: Hendrickson, 2002).

12. For a profound treatment of "wrestling with" the biblical text, see Phyllis Trible, "Take Back the Bible," *Review & Expositor* 97 (2000): 425–31.

13. Zenger, *A God of Vengeance?* 11.

14. Ibid., 20–22.

15. Ibid., 9.

16. Othmar Keel, *Feinde und Gottesleugner. Studien zum Image der Widersacher in den Individualpsalmen* (SBM 7; Stuttgart: Verlag Katholisches Bibelwerk, 1969), 93–131.

17. Psalms 69, 94, and 109 are categorized as individual laments.

18. Zenger, *A God of Vengeance?* 66.

19. John Mark Hicks, "Preaching Community Laments: Responding to Disillusionment with God and Injustice in the World," in *Performing the Psalms* (ed. David Fleer and David Bland; St. Louis: Chalice, 2005), 75–76.

20. Walter Brueggemann, "The Costly Loss of Lament," in *The Psalms and the Life of Faith* (ed. Patrick D. Miller; Minneapolis: Fortress Press, 1995), 105.

21. J. Clinton McCann Jr., *A Theological Introduction to the Book of Psalms: The Psalms as Torah* (Nashville: Abingdon, 1993), 119–20.

22. Patrick D. Miller, "The Hermeneutics of Imprecation," in *Theology in the Service of the Church: Essays in Honor of Thomas W. Gillespie* (ed. Wallace M. Alston Jr.; Grand Rapids: Eerdmans, 2000), 162.

23. Zenger, *A God of Vengeance?* 48.

Chapter 6: Saying Amen to Violent Psalms

1. Gordon Wenham has noted this tendency in two recent articles: "The Ethics of the Psalms," in *Interpreting the Psalms: Issues and Approaches* (ed. Philip S. Johnson and David G. Firth; Downers Grove, Ill.: IVP Academic, 2005), 175–94; and "Prayer and Practice in the Psalms," in *Psalms and Prayers: Papers Read at the Joint Meeting of the Society of Old Testament Study and Het Oudtestamentische Werkgezelschap in Nederland in Apeldoorn, 21–24 August 2006* (ed. Bob Becking and Eric Peels; OTS 55; Leiden: Brill, 2007), 279–95. These two essays represent important steps in identifying the place of the Psalms within biblical ethics. A study of Psalmic ethics with a very different tone than Wenham's also deserves mention here: David J. A. Clines's "Psalm 2 and the MLF (Moabite Liberation Front)," in *The Bible in Human Society: Essays in Honour of John Rogerson* (ed. M. Daniel Carroll R., David J. A. Clines, and Philip R. Davies; JSOTSup 200; Sheffield: Sheffield Academic, 1995), 158–85.

2. Of the many important treatments of the nexus between prayer and belief (i.e., theology), see especially Patrick Miller, *They Cried to the Lord: The Form and Theology of Biblical Prayer* (Minneapolis: Fortress Press, 1994), 1: "Theologians have long maintained that theology is at least in part an outgrowth of prayer . . . that it is not simply a matter of believing and then praying to God in light of what one believes. That very belief is shaped by the practice of prayer. So prayer and theology exist in relation to each other in a correcting circle, the one learning from the other and correcting the other."

3. The phrase is attributed to Prosper of Aquitaine, appearing in *Indicu-lus*, written 435–442. See Paul DeClerk, " 'Lex orandi, lex credendi:' Sens original et avatars historiques d'un adage équivoque," *Questions liturgiques* 59 (1978): 194–96.

4. Geoffrey Wainwright, *Doxology: The Praise of God in Worship, Doc-trine, and Life: A Systematic Theology* (New York: Oxford University Press, 1984); Don E. Saliers, *Worship as Theology: Foretaste of Glory Divine* (Nash-ville: Abingdon, 1994), 187. L. Edward Phillips, "Liturgy and Ethics," in *Liturgy in Dialogue: Essays in Memory of Ronald Jasper* (ed. Paul Bradshaw and Bryan Spinks; Collegeville, Minn.: Liturgical, 1995), 86–99.

5. I use the phrase "moral imagination" in its most simple sense here, as the way individuals and communities create series of images to construct systems of equity within the world. On the use of the term within biblical ethics see William P. Brown, *The Ethos of the Cosmos: The Genesis of Moral Imagination in the Hebrew Bible* (Grand Rapids: Eerdmans, 1999), 19–23.

6. Unless noted, all Scripture citations in this essay follow the NRSV.

7. On the importance of the creation myth for the formulation of eth-ics in the Psalms and in the broader ancient Near East, see Eckart Otto, "Myth and Hebrew Ethics in the Psalms," in *Psalms and Mythology* (ed. Dirk J. Human; New York: T & T Clark, 2007), 26–37.

8. See J. Clinton McCann Jr., *A Theological Introduction to the Book of Psalms: The Psalms as Torah* (Nashville: Abingdon, 1993), 27. Noting the correspondence between the structures of the Torah and the Psalms does not necessitate the argument that the fivefold division of the Psalter reflects a particular lectionary cycle whereby psalms from book one cor-respond to Genesis, book two to Exodus, and so on. See Gerald H. Wil-son, *The Editing of the Hebrew Psalter* (SBLDS 76; Chico, Calif.: Scholars, 1985), 200–203.

9. Wenham, "The Ethics of the Psalms," 179–87.

10. See James Luther Mays, "The Place of the Torah-Psalms in the Psalter," *JBL* 106 (1987): 3–12.

11. See ibid.; McCann, *Theological Introduction*, 25–40.

12. Michael LeFebvre, "Torah-Meditation and the Psalms: The Invi-tation of Psalm 1," in *Interpreting the Psalms: Issues and Approaches* (ed. Philip S. Johnson and David G. Firth; Downers Grove, Ill.: IVP Aca-demic, 2005), 213–25. See also Athanase Negoiță and Helmer Ringgern, "*Hāgāh*," *TDOT* 3:321–24.

13. Erich Zenger has helpfully outlined a number of the proposals. See Erich Zenger, *A God of Vengeance? Understanding the Psalms of Divine Wrath* (trans. Linda M. Maloney; Louisville: Westminster John Knox,

1996), 13–23. For an even more recent summary of proposals, see Brent A. Strawn, "Imprecation," in *Dictionary of the Old Testament: Wisdom, Poetry and Writings* (ed. Tremper Longman III and Peter Enns; Downers Grove, Ill.: IVP Academic, 2008), 314–20.

14. United Methodist Church, *The United Methodist Hymnal: Book of United Methodist Worship* (Nashville: United Methodist Publishing House, 1989); Presbyterian Church (U.S.A.), *The Presbyterian Hymnal: Hymns, Psalms, and Spiritual Songs* (Louisville: Westminster John Knox, 1990).

15. Consultation on Common Texts, *The Revised Common Lectionary 1992: The Report from the Consultation on Common Texts* (Nashville: Abingdon, 1992).

16. W. O. E. Oesterley, *The Psalms* (London: SPCK, 1962), 549.

17. Artur Weiser, *The Psalms: A Commentary* (trans. Herbert Hartwell; OTL; Philadelphia: Westminster, 1962), 432.

18. To this end, Zenger cites several illustrative passages from the commentaries by Bernhard Duhm and Artur Weiser (Zenger, *A God of Vengeance*, 14).

19. Zenger notes explicitly Marcionite comments appearing in essays by Heinrich Junker, Emanuel Hirsch, Friedrich Baumgärtel (Zenger, *A God of Vengeance*, 17–19).

20. Ibid., 18.

21. See, recently, Anders Gerdmar, *Roots of Theological Anti-Semitism: German Biblical Interpretation and the Jews, from Herder and Semler to Kittel and Bultmann* (Studies in Jewish History and Culture 20; Leiden: Brill, 2009).

22. A movement motivated in large part by Walter Brueggemann. See idem, "Psalms and the Life of Faith: A Suggested Typology of Function," in *The Psalms and the Life of Faith* (ed. Patrick D. Miller; Minneapolis: Fortress, 1995), 1–32.

23. McCann, *Theological Introduction*, 115.

24. Patrick D. Miller, *The Way of the Lord: Essays in Old Testament Theology* (Grand Rapids: Eerdmans, 2007), 200.

25. Zenger, *A God of Vengeance*, vii.

26. David G. Firth, *Surrendering Retribution in the Psalms: Responses to Violence in Individual Complaints* (Paternoster Biblical Monographs; Eugene, Ore.: Wipf and Stock, 2007), 142.

27. Ibid., 141.

28. Ellen F. Davis, *Getting Involved with God: Rediscovering the Old Testament* (Cambridge, Mass.: Cowley, 2001), 28.

29. Erhard S. Gerstenberger, "Enemies and Evildoers in the Psalms: A Challenge to Christian Preaching," *HBT* 4 (1983): 77.

30. Roland E. Murphy, *The Psalms, Job* (Philadelphia: Fortress Press, 1977), 29.

31. My translation. For a discussion of the manifold text-critical and translational issues in these verses, see Joel M. LeMon, *Yahweh's Winged Form in the Psalms: Exploring Congruent Iconography and Texts* (OBO; Fribourg: Academic; Göttingen: Vandenhoeck and Ruprecht, 2010), 62–67.

32. Firth understands the following to be the psalms of the individual that relate images of violence: Pss 3, 7, 17, 27, 35, 38, 55–56, 64, 69, 109, 139, 143 (*Surrendering Retribution*, 11–15).

33. In a response against Zenger's "efforts to justify these prayers," James L. Crenshaw argues that "religious people tend to identify their own enemies with God's adversaries. . . . The use of the Psalms for daily devotion and as a model for prayer therefore runs the risk of infecting religious people with harmful attitudes" (*The Psalms: An Introduction* [Grand Rapids: Eerdmans, 2001], 68).

34. Bob Allen, "Former SBC Officer Says Tiller Murder Answer to Prayer," *Associated Baptist Press*, June 2, 2009, http://www.abpnews.com/index.php?option=com_content&task=view&id=4119&Itemid=53.

35. Bob Allen, "Drake, Former SBC Officer, Says He's Praying for Obama to Die (updated)," *Associated Baptist Press*, June 3, 2009, http://www.abpnews.com/index.php?option=com_content&task=view&id=4126&Itemid=53.

36. Ibid.

37. The literature on blessings and curses in the Hebrew Bible is, of course, quite extensive. For a recent review of scholarship, see J. K. Aitken, *The Semantics of Blessing and Cursing in Ancient Hebrew* (Ancient Near Eastern Studies Supplement 23; Louvain: Peeters, 2007), esp. 1–41.

Chapter 7: "The Faithfulness of the Lord Endures Forever"

1. Recent attempts to articulate a theology of the Psalter include James Luther Mays, Jerome F. D. Creach, William Brown, and Hermann Spieckermann. Mays asserts that the confession "The Lord reigns" is the center of the Psalter (*The Lord Reigns: A Theological Handbook to the Psalms* [Louisville: Westminster John Knox, 1994]). Creach argues that the metaphor of God as "refuge" is the theological center of the Psalter (*Yahweh as Refuge and the Editing of the Hebrew Psalter* [Sheffield: Sheffield Academic,

1996]). Brown builds on Creach's work and argues that the metaphors of God as "refuge" and "way" work together to form the theological center of the Psalms (*Seeing the Psalms: A Theology of Metaphor* [Louisville: Westminster John Knox, 2002]). Gerald Wilson argues that the reign of God is the center of the Psalter's theology ("Psalms and the Psalter: Paradigm for Biblical Theology," in *Biblical Theology: Retrospect and Prospect* (ed. S. J. Hafemann; Downers Grove, Ill.: Intervarsity, 2002). Hermann Spieckermann argues that the presence of God's salvation is both the theological problem that drives the Psalter's theology and the answer to that problem (*Heilgegenwart: Eine Theologie der Psalmen* [Göttingen: Vandenhoeck and Ruprecht, 1989]; see his survey of recent approaches to the theology of the Psalter on 7–20); Robert Foster ("*Topoi* of Praise in the Call to Praise Psalms," in *My Words are Lovely: Studies in the Rhetoric of the Psalms* [ed. R. Foster and D. Howard; London: T & T Clark, 2008], 75–88) applies a rhetorical approach to the question, suggesting that the calls to praise in the praise psalms point to basic characteristics of the Lord; he briefly mentions God's faithfulness but does not advance the argument beyond the conclusions of Mays and Wilson.

2. Von Rad, *Old Testament Theology*, 2:372n6.

3. In *Melanchthon and Bucer* (ed. W. Pauck; Library of Christian Classics; Philadelphia: Westminster, 1969), 21–22.

4. The above family of terms that are used to describe God—with an emphasis on the two primary terms *ḥesed* and *ʾĕmet*—together paint a picture of a God who is faithful in relationship. The terms will draw us to specific texts that can be investigated in order to understand precisely what the Psalter means by God's faithfulness and how it understands God's faithfulness to be experienced and made available.

5. Regarding creation, the psalm bears witness first to God's originating creative acts—the Lord "made the heavens" and "spread out the earth on the waters" (vv. 5–6); the psalm also bears witness to God's sustaining creative acts—the Lord's creations of sun and moon to "rule over the day" and "over the night" (the verb *māšal* here implying the sustaining creative acts of ordering or governing) and the Lord "gives food to all flesh" (v. 25). Regarding this history of the Lord's gracious acts on behalf of Israel, the psalm testifies to the Lord's delivering victory over Egypt (vv. 10-15), the guidance through the wilderness (vv. 16-20), and the gift of the land (vv. 21-22). It is, of course, not new to point out the fact that this psalm or the Psalter as a whole confesses faith in God as both Creator and Lord of history. Rather, the point I wish to stress is the connection between these acts and the psalm's confession that the Lord is a God of *ḥesed*. Over

and over—literally, over and over twenty-six times—the psalm makes the connection between these actions of God (who by understanding made the heavens, who remembered us in our low estate, and so on) and God's characteristic fidelity—for his steadfast love endures forever. The psalm treats each of God's actions that it attributes to God as a reason to conclude that God's character is one of faithfulness. We could turn the rhetoric of the psalm verses and responses into a protasis-apodosis relationship: If you acknowledge that the Lord "remembered us in our low estate," then you must agree that the Lord is a God of faithfulness; if you acknowledge that the Lord "gives food to all flesh," then you must agree that the Lord is a God of faithfulness. And so on.

6. See Claus Westermann, *The Psalms: Structure, Content and Message* (Minneapolis: Augsburg Publishing House, 1980), 93–96.

7. See Diane Jacobson, "Psalm 33 and the Creation Rhetoric of a Torah Psalm," in *My Words are Lovely: Studies in the Rhetoric of the Psalms* (ed. R. Foster and D. Howard; London: T & T Clark, 2008), 91–106; Terence Fretheim, *God and World in the Old Testament: A Relational Theology of Creation* (Nashville: Abingdon, 2005).

8. The terms *bitbûnâ* and *běḥokmâ* here refer not merely to God's means of creating but even more to God's design in and purpose for creation.

9. Notice that the progression from domesticated animals (sheep and oxen) through increasingly more wild spheres of undomesticated animals (from beasts to birds to fish) suggests a natural order in creation.

10. The choice of the term "rule" reflects the Psalter's language. Examples include: "You divided the sea by your might" (74:13; cf 78:13), "You rule the raging of the sea" (89:10), "He gathered the waters of the sea as in a bottle" (33:7), as well as language that describes the sea and waters and depths as afraid of God and fleeing from God (cf. 77:16; 114:5-6).

11. The Psalms' witness to God's faithful character as revealed in creation is worth stressing—the fact that human beings cannot fully perceive, understand, or grasp it. To say this another way, if the Psalms are clear that creation bears testimony to God's fidelity, then the Psalms are equally clear that human beings are incapable of grasping the full witness of creation. Which means, among other things, that human beings will not be able fully to understand God's faithfulness. Psalm 19 says, "Day to day pours forth speech, and night to night declares knowledge. *There is no speech, nor are there words; their voice is not heard*; yet their voice goes out through all the earth, and their words to the end of the world" (vv. 3-4). Nature's testimony to God's faithfulness comes through to human beings like a mumbled conversation, in a foreign tongue, heard through muffled

insulation of a closed door. We are aware of it, even aware of it significance, but much or even most is simply beyond us. Psalm 139 acknowledges that "such knowledge is too wonderful for me; it is so high that I cannot attain it" (v. 6). That it will be important to heed this warning will be apparent later, when we consider the challenge that the psalms of lament pose when they question God's character and call it into doubt. So even as the Psalter bears witness that through creation God is faithful to those with whom God is in relationship, the Psalter is also clear that those creatures have a limited capacity to grasp what it means for God to be Creator or to be faithful.

12. Peter C. Craigie, *Psalms 1–50* (WBC; Dallas: Word, 1983), 200. Although it should be noted that Craigie does imagine the psalm as a liturgy for someone suffering from disease.

13. Ibid., 261.

14. The eye wasting away is a Hebrew idiom indicating decline and weakness. Moses' aged vitality is indicated by the fact that his eyesight did not fail (Deut 34:7). In Pss 6 and 31, the failing eyesight is both a literal reference to failing health but also a cipher for generally failing health. See also Ps 88:8.

15. In those documents, Israel seems aware that Israel's need for a human monarchy is prima facie evidence that Israel has rejected God (1 Sam 8:7). Israel is also aware that the reign of an unfaithful king exponentially multiplies the suffering of the people. On the other hand, Israel is aware that good government (and in the ancient world this means a good king) was a blessing.

16. Recently, Psalms scholars exploring the meaning of the "shape and shaping" of the Hebrew Psalter have argued that the Psalter has a critical view of the Davidic covenant (and thus the Davidic kings). The basis of this argument is the placement of Psalm 89, which laments what some describe as the failure of the Davidic covenant, at the end of book 3 of the Psalter. Book 4 then begins with Psalm 90, which is the only psalm of Moses. See especially Gerald H. Wilson *The Editing of the Hebrew Psalter* (Chico, Calif.: Scholars, 1985); and Nancy L. deClaissé-Walford, *Reading from the Beginning: The Shaping of the Hebrew Psalter* (Macon, Ga.: Mercer University Press, 1997); idem, "The Canonical Shape of the Psalms," in *An Introduction to Wisdom Literature and the Psalms: Festschrift Marvin E. Tate* (ed. H. W. Ballard Jr. and W. D. Tucker Jr.; Macon, Ga.: Mercer University Press, 2000), 93–110; and idem, *Introduction to the Psalms: A Song from Ancient Israel* (St. Louis: Chalice, 2004). But many psalms of David follow, including many that are panegyrics toward the

king, so I do not share the conclusion that the Psalter is critical toward the Davidic throne.

17. The Psalter also depicts the king as the human whose relationship with God is paradigmatic of the divine-human relationship. The Lord's promises to David are not only indicative of the Davidic covenant; they are understood as a fulcrum on which the Lord's relationship with the entire people pivots. When Psalm 89 laments the apparent abrogation of the Davidic covenant, its cry of pain is spoken not merely on behalf of the Davidic monarch (perhaps Jehoiachin or Zedekiah) whose reign was interrupted but on behalf of the entire people who suffer as well. Likewise, when Psalm 132 celebrates the Lord's oath to David, it celebrates David's election as a blessing for the poor, who are provided with bread. Thus, the monarchy is more than merely an important institution; it is seen as a means of divine faithfulness.

18. Hans-Joachim Kraus, *Theology of the Psalms* (trans. Keith Crim; Minneapolis: Augsburg, 1986), 59.

19. The first psalm of the Psalter offers two initial promises to the reader/listener. The psalm promises both that those who transplant their lives so as to sink their roots into the Word of God will prosper and also that they will find a faithful community to join—a "congregation of righteous people." More on the former promise momentarily; for now I will address the latter promise, that there is a community of righteousness for those who are beleaguered by the wicked.

As many commentators have noted, the metaphor of the "way" is integral to Psalm 1. This is most certainly true. But it should also be noted that the emphasis is not so much on the way itself as on *whose* way. The poem teaches us to be like the righteous, whose way is to meditate on God's word constantly (more on that later), rather than like the wicked, whose advice leads to destruction. The point is that wicked and the righteous are two contrasting people in the community; the wicked and righteous constitute two different modes of actualizing human community. And when it comes to the difference between the two, God is not neutral—God is at work to create a community of righteousness that can serve as refuge from and bulwark against the wicked.

20. Jerome F. D. Creach, *The Destiny of the Righteous in the Psalms* (St. Louis: Chalice, 2008), 29.

21. Psalm 2 begins immediately by describing the dangerous elements of human community: "Why do the nations conspire, and the peoples plot in vain? The kings of the earth set themselves, and the rulers take counsel together, against the Lord and his anointed" (vv. 1-2a). The second psalm

thus echoes a basic concern of the first psalm by naming the rebellious, chaotic forces of the world as the enemies of both God's people and of God—the nations rebel "against the Lord and his anointed." The poetic structure of Psalm 2 is both elegant and revealing. The poem has four stanzas of almost identical length, which have an A-B-B'-A' pattern: the first and last stanzas feature "the king" and "rulers." The middle two stanzas feature the Lord and "his anointed." With each stanza, the location of the action changes. Each of the first three stanzas closes with a quotation, and a different speaker speaks each quotation. The last stanza lacks a closing quotation, but the "kings and rulers" who had spoken rebelliously against the Lord in the first stanza now bow in humble silence.

The structure of the psalm highlights the underappreciated fact that in this psalm nobody does anything other than speak. Different characters conspire, plot, laugh, deride, speak, say, and tell. The nations/kings rebel against the Lord by speaking: "Let us burst their bonds asunder." The Lord answers that rebellion with a contrasting speech: "I have set my king on Zion, my holy hill." The king likewise responds to the rebellion by reciting the spoken promise of the Lord: "He said to me, 'You are my son.'" Then, in the final stanza, the narrating voice warns the rebelling rulers to serve the Lord and to silence their mouths with the humble action of a kiss.

The centrality of the speech motif in Psalm 2 is similar to the tree-*torah* metaphor in Psalm 1. Whereas in Psalm 1 both the originating power to become and the sustaining power to remain a member of the righteous are found in the living water of the word, so in Psalm 2 it is the sheer spoken word that funds the king's resilience in the face of global rebellion. Just as the solitary "one" (*'îš*) of the first psalm is promised that in the Torah she will find the source to resist the multiple foes (the wicked, sinners, and scoffers) who beset her, so the solitary king of the second psalm is given a promise from the Lord that he finds as the source that allows him to resist the multiple foes (the nations/people, kings of earth/rulers) that beset him.

22. Thanks to my colleague Terence Fretheim for suggesting the distinction between office and person in relation to the Psalter's confession as the king as a means of God's faithfulness.

Chapter 8: Rethinking the Enterprise

1. John Collins notes, "The so-called biblical theology movement, which tried gallantly to combine progressive historical scholarship with confessional faith, died of its own contradictions in the late 1960's" ("Biblical

Theology of the Old and New Testaments: Theological Reflection on the Christian Bible," *Christian Century*, July 28, 1993, 743.

2. This center or core was championed by Walther Eichrodt, who argued the Old Testament is "a self-contained entity exhibiting, despite ever-changing historical condition, a constant basic tendency and character," *Theology of the Old Testament* (trans. J. A. Baker; Philadelphia: Westminster, 1961), 1:11. Gerhard von Rad also argued for a center of *Heilsgeschichte*, or salvation history, *Old Testament Theology*, vol 1: *The Theology of Israel's Historical Traditions* (trans. D. Stalker; New York: Harper and Row, 1967).

3. Erhard Gerstenberger, "Theologies in the Book of Psalms," in *Book of Psalms: Composition and Reception* (ed. P. Flint and P. Miller; Leiden: Brill, 2005), 603.

4. James Sanders, *From Sacred Story to Sacred Text* (Philadelphia: Fortress Press, 1984).

5. On the one hand, the ancient witnesses provide a multitude of books (or scrolls) of the Psalms. There are different superscriptions, order, and even numbering in these ancient witnesses, reminding us that while we often speak of the text, what we really mean are the texts. Yet for most purposes, when we speak of the book of Psalms today, we mean the one that appears in the Protestant and Jewish publications of 150 psalms or the Catholic publication of 151 psalms. Carl Bosma rightly refers to this as "the *Sitz-im-Buch* of a psalm"; "Discerning the Voices in the Psalms: A Discussion of the *Two* Problems in Psalmic Interpretation," *Calvin Theological Journal* 44 (2009): 155.

6. Gerald Wilson, *The Editing of the Hebrew Psalter* (Chico, Calif.: Scholars), 1985.

7. The book *The Power of Positive Thinking* by Norman Vincent Peale is one of a plethora of examples of this theology. The book was first printed in 1952 by Prentice Hall.

8. Some of the scholarly offerings are Sally Brown and Patrick Miller, eds., *Lament: Reclaiming Practices in Pulpit, Pew, and Public Square* (Louisville: Westminster John Knox, 2005); and Kathleen Biullman and Daniel Migliore, *Rachel's Cry: Prayers of Lament and the Rebirth of Hope* (Cleveland: United Church Press, 1999). Also there are more resources available for the general public: Michael Card, *A Sacred Sorrow Experience Guide: Reaching Out to God in the Lost Language of Lament.* (Colorado Springs: NavPress, 2005); and Teresa Smith, *Through the Darkest Valley: The Lament Psalms and One Woman's Lifelong Battle Against Depression* (Eugene, Ore.: Resource Publications, 2009).

9. Walter Brueggemann, "*Theology of the Old Testament*: A Prompt Retrospect," in *God in the Fray: A Tribute to Walter Brueggemann* (ed. T. Linafelt and T. Beal; Minneapolis: Fortress Press, 1998), 307.

10. This assumption of the innate historicity of biblical narratives has been under critical analysis in recent years and ironically has led to a narrowing of the gap between these two genres; see Lester Grabbe, *Ancient Israel: What Do We Know and How Do We Know It?* (New York: T & T Clark, 2007).

11. In commentaries from 1940–1980, it was not uncommon for psalms to be cut into two different psalms or for scholars to rearrange verses to make sense of the difficult prose from our perspective, implying our ways of thinking were superior to the ancients who first created and used these works. See for example the division of Psalms 19 and 55 into two different psalms in Hans-Joachim Kraus, *Psalms 1–59* and *Psalms 60–150* (trans. H. Oswald; Minneapolis: Augusbug Press, 1988, 1989). Also William Foxwell Albright argues Psalm 68 is not a psalm at all but a collection of titles of other psalms, "A Catalogue of Early Hebrew Lyric Poems (Psalms 68)," *HUCA* 23 (1950–51): 1–39.

12. Solomon Snyder, "Seeking God in the Brain—Efforts to Localize Higher Brain Function," *New England Journal of Medicine* 358, no. 1 (January 2008): 6–7.

13. Jane Elliott, "How Singing Unlocks the Brain," BBC News, November 20, 2005, http://news.bbc.co.uk/2/hi/health/4448634.stm.

14. Patrick Miller, *Interpreting the Psalms* (Philadelphia: Fortress Press, 1986), 22.

15. Gerald Wilson, "Psalms and the Psalter: Paradigm for Biblical Theology," in *Biblical Theology: Retrospect and Prospect* (ed. S. Hafemann; Downers Grove, Ill.: Intervarsity, 2002), 100.

16. Meir Sternberg, *The Poetics of Biblical Narrative* (Bloomington: Indiana University Press, 1987).

17. Sternberg, *Poetics*, 187.

18. Wilson, "Psalms and the Psalter," 102.

19. Miller, *Interpreting the Psalms*, 19.

20. Carl Bosma, "Discerning the Voices in the Psalms: A Discussion of Two Problems in Psalmic Interpretation, Part 2," *Calvin Theological Journal* 44 (2009): 127–70.

Author Index

Biblical Index